lo

POCKET
BUDAPEST

Kata Fári & Steve Fallon

Contents

Top: Street food, Budapest
Bottom: Fisherman's Bastion (p42)

Plan Your Trip 4

The Journey Begins Here	4
Our Picks	6
Perfect Days	16
Get Prepared	20
When To Go	22
Getting There	24
Getting Around	25
A Few Surprises	28

POCKET **BUDAPEST**

Explore Budapest 31

Castle District	33
Gellért Hill & Tabán	49
Óbuda & the Buda Hills	65
Belváros	77
Parliament & Around	87
Margaret Island & Northern Pest	101
Erzsébetváros & the Jewish Quarter	111
Southern Pest	127

Budapest Toolkit 143

Family Travel	144
Accommodation	145
Food, Drink & Nightlife	146
LGBTIQ+ Travellers	148
Health & Safe Travel	149
Responsible Travel	150
Accessible Travel	152
Nuts & Bolts	153
Language	154
Index	156

FROM TOP LEFT: TSUGULIEV/SHUTTERSTOCK ©, ZGPHOTOGRAPHY/SHUTTERSTOCK ©

★ Top Experiences

Royal Palace	36
Gellért Baths	52
Gellért Hill & Liberty Monument	54
Memento Park	62
Aquincum	68
Children's Railway	69
Parliament	90
Basilica of St Stephen	92
Margaret Island	103
Great Synagogue	114
House of Terror	115
Holocaust Memorial Centre	129
Hungarian National Museum	130
City Park	138

PLAN YOUR TRIP

The Journey Begins Here

Know that sudden gush of love you get when you look at somebody you've known forever, but for a split second, realise again just how beautiful they are? This happens every time I cross a bridge in Budapest. My love story with the city has seen splashes at stunning spas, nights lost at random ruin bars, hikes through the Buda Hills, books read at century-old coffeehouses and romantic boat trips on the Danube. I love Budapest because it's elegant, historic, bohemian and random all at once, and even though I know it like the back of my hand, it still manages to surprise me time and again. – *Kata Fári*

Kata Fári
@kata.fari
Kata is a member of our diverse team of travel experts from around the world. She is based in Budapest and sings the praises of the world's best places online and in print.

Steve Fallon
steveslondon.com
Steve is a travel writer and qualified London Blue Badge Tourist Guide. He's a prolific Lonely Planet contributor and has worked on every edition of our Budapest and Hungary guides.

Szimpla Kert (p124)
ANDRES NAGA/SHUTTERSTOCK ©

THE BEST

Thermal Baths

Its famously elegant and splendid bathhouses make Budapest the 'World's Spa Capital', where you can plunge into a thermal pool and soak away your stress and worries in warm, muscle-melting, mineral-rich waters.

Picture sunflower-yellow walls surrounding steaming outdoor pools, and the sight of old chaps playing chess in the water – **Széchenyi Baths** are as epic as their hype. (pictured; p139)

Head to the rooftop hot tub with a pretty view of the Pest skyline at **Rudas Baths**, standing since Hungary's Turkish conquest and featuring single-sex days and weekend nighttime bathing. (p58)

See an Art Nouveau masterpiece, **Gellért Baths**, where bathing feels like a royal ritual. (pictured; p52)

Heal at local **Lukács Baths**, offering a peaceful escape from the city's more crowded tourist spots. (p73)

Soak at **Veli Bej Baths**, less crowded than the big-name baths and a venerable choice combining historic charm with modern comforts. (p73)

Right: **Széchenyi Baths** (p139)

THE BEST

Major Museums

Set in amazing buildings that are worth a visit alone, Budapest's museums explore the art and history of Hungary and beyond.

See the most important works of Hungarian art at the **Hungarian National Gallery**. (p36)

Find outstanding foreign artworks from the likes of Raphael, El Greco and Goya at the **Museum of Fine Arts**. (p138)

Witness the rise of anti-Semitism in Hungary, leading to the genocide of Jewish and Roma communities at the **Holocaust Memorial Centre**. (p129)

Trace the history of the Magyar people and Hungary from the 9th-century conquest to the fall of communism at the **National Museum**. (p130)

Explore centuries of music history, from shamanic drumming to movie scores, at the **House of Music**. (p141)

Learn about the history of Budapest from ancient times to the present day at the **Castle Museum**. (p37)

Museum of Fine Arts (p138)

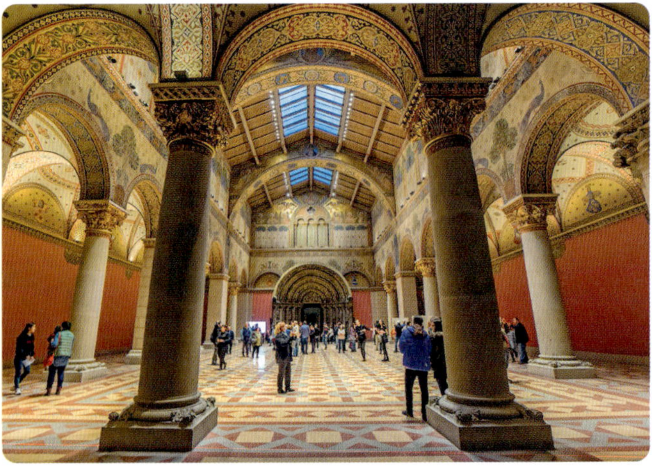

ANDOCS/SHUTTERSTOCK ©

THE BEST

Nightlife Spots

From random ruin bars to sky-high rooftop spots and delightful wine bars, there are endless places to enjoy Budapest's buzzing, quirky and fun nightlife. Any of these could be a great starting point.

Experience the Budapest phenomenon of ruin bars in ramshackle buildings, from the patriarch of them all, **Szimpla Kert** (pictured), to ever-so-quirky **Csendes Létterem** and hip **Púder Bárszínház**. (p124)

Party till dawn at **Instant-Fogas**, where two ruin bars have merged to become the biggest in town, with dozens of rooms in which to get lost. (p124)

Find clubs, karaoke, Hungarian wine, tapas and more at **Gozsdu Courtyard**, the city's ever-lively nightlife spot. (pictured; p121)

Admire out-of-this-world views at hip rooftop **360 Bar**. For equally outstanding views but smaller crowds, try **St Andrea Skybar**. (p125)

Catch a gig at the city's coolest concert venue, **A38**, on a decommissioned Ukrainian cargo ship. (p60)

THE BEST

Historic Landmarks

Though all of Budapest is downright beautiful, some historic landmarks and monuments stand out as real crowd-pleasers that must be seen when in town.

Marvel at the crown jewel of Castle Hill, the **Royal Palace**, towering over Budapest with a commanding presence. (pictured; p36)

Take a tour to admire the **Parliament**, one of the city's finest architectural landmarks, home to artworks and the Holy Crown of Hungary. (p90)

See Hungary's most revered relic, the mummified hand of King St Stephen, at the **Basilica of St Stephen**. (p92)

Enjoy a crash course in Hungarian history at the city's most emblematic square, **Heroes' Square**. It's especially majestic at night. (pictured; p138)

Take photos at fairy-tale-like **Fisherman's Bastion**, providing a pretty panorama over the Pest skyline. (p42)

Join one of the daily tours at the neo-Renaissance **Hungarian State Opera House**, stunning inside and out. (p97)

Right: Fisherman's Bastion (p42)

PLAN YOUR TRIP

THE BEST

Outdoor Experiences

Whether you like walks in groomed gardens, hikes on picturesque hills, spelunking, screaming on a speedboat or dipping your toes in the Danube with a drink in hand, Budapest has it all.

Stroll around lovely **Margaret Island**, with its huge green areas, swimming complexes, a thermal spa, gardens and centuries-old ruins. (p101)

Enjoy hiking trails and viewpoints in the **Buda Hills**, home to Budapest's highest point. (pictured; p72)

Take a ride on **RedJet**, a speedboat zooming by the capital's most splendid sights at 80km/h. (p58)

Settle into **City Park**, a heavyweight for sights, but also offering endless picnic spots, sports facilities, playgrounds and a jogging track. (p138)

Embark on fascinating tours to see dripstones and crystals at natural caves such as **Pál-völgy** or **Szemlő-hegy**. (p72)

Relax by the riverside at **Római-part** on the city's northern outskirts, known for its lovely laid-back atmosphere. (pictured; p74)

Ice-skating, Városliget Lake (p140)

THE BEST
Winter Wonderlands

Santa Claus comes early in Hungary (6 December) and Budapest is in a festive mood during the whole month with Christmas markets, ice-skating rinks and fairy lights all around the city.

Visit the best Christmas market in town at central **Vörösmarty tér**, where wooden kiosks sell handmade gifts and iconic wintertime treats and various events take place – the Finnish Joulupukki (Christmas goat) even pays a visit. (p144)

Enjoy light shows projected onto the facade of the **Basilica of St Stephen** after dark during the Basilica Advent Fair. (p92)

Have a merry ride on scenic **tram 2**, which in December dons festive decor and is covered in hundreds of LED lights as it passes by the city's most gorgeous sights. (p25)

Lace up your skates at **Városliget Lake** in City Park, which turns into Europe's largest outdoor ice-skating rink in winter, enhanced with fairy lights, mulled wine and atmospheric music. (p140)

Memento Park (p62)

THE BEST

Communist Mementos

Budapest still has sites that reflect Hungary's experience under Soviet influence from the end of WWII through the 1956 Uprising to the fall of the Iron Curtain in 1989.

See statues of communist leaders and propaganda removed from Budapest's streets at **Memento Park**. (p62)

See the wreathed hammer and sickle and large gold star of Szabadság tér's **Soviet Army Memorial**. (p95)

Learn about Hungary's post-WWII history at the harrowing **House of Terror**, inside the former headquarters of the communist secret police. (p115)

Stroll around **Kerepesi Cemetery** to see the huge Workers' Movement Pantheon and the grave of former communist leader János Kádár, desecrated in 2007 – his skull is still missing. (p134)

Discover what life was like in Budapest during Soviet times at the fun **Retro Museum**. See a typical home or sit inside a Lada. (p97)

Shop at **Ecseri Piac**, which sells everything from propaganda posters to Soviet army watches. (p135)

Best for Kids

Time your visit around the many feeding sessions, and see nearly 1000 species of animals, at the enormous **Budapest Zoo**. (p140)

Zoom past some of the Buda Hills' best excursion spots on the **Children's Railway**, staffed almost entirely by kids in cute uniforms. (p69)

Wander around **City Park** to find many cool playgrounds, including a traffic park where little ones can learn the rules of the road. (p138)

Ride the large **Ferris Wheel of Budapest** for stunning views of Pest and across the Danube to Buda. It's particularly impressive at night. (p82)

Make a splash at **Aquaworld**, one of Europe's largest water parks, housing pools with slides and an array of saunas to keep the whole family at play year-round. (p103)

Best for Free

Enjoy the lovely short hike on a meandering forested path to the top of **Gellért Hill**, one of the best viewpoints in Budapest. (p54)

Take the Royal Steps to the **Royal Palace** to stroll around the grounds and gardens, enjoying wonderful monuments and incredible views. (p36)

See the city's emblematic **Heroes' Square**, which is especially striking at night. (p138)

Walk along the **Duna Korzó** for views of landmarks such as the Parliament, Chain Bridge and Royal Palace. (p81)

Snap photos from **Fisherman's Bastion** – only the upstairs viewing platform requires a ticket. (p42)

Perfect Days

Astonishing architecture, healing thermal baths, buzzing nightlife and old-world charm mingling with modern vibes – this is why you come to Budapest. Knock back a coffee like a local before hitting the streets.

DAY ONE

Only Have One Day?

MORNING

Spend your morning on Castle Hill admiring the views from the **Royal Palace** (p36) and **Fisherman's Bastion** (p42). There are several museums up here, but choose either the **Hungarian National Gallery** (p39) for fine art or the **Castle Museum** (p37) for an introduction to the city's storied past.

AFTERNOON

After lunch, climb **Gellért Hill** (p54) for a panorama and to see the city's iconic **Liberty Monument** (p54). Then soak any tired muscles at mesmerising **Gellért Baths** (p52).

EVENING

End the day with a night Danube cruise (pictured) to get front-row seats to the illuminated **Parliament** (p90), Royal Palace, **Chain Bridge** (p42) and other landmarks.

View from Fisherman's Bastion (p42)

DAY TWO
A Weekend Trip

MORNING
Stroll along leafy Andrássy út, past the **Hungarian State Opera House** (p97), to **Heroes' Square** (p138) and **City Park** (p138), or ride the charmingly retro **Millennium Underground** (p82) for a quicker trip.

AFTERNOON
For an educational afternoon, go for the harrowing **House of Terror** (pictured; p115) or the astonishing **Museum of Fine Arts** (p138). For a leisurely afternoon, head to City Park for the **Budapest Zoo** (p140) or **Széchenyi Baths** (p139).

EVENING
Check out one of Budapest's historic coffeehouses such as the **New York Café** (p120), then get lost in Erzsébetváros' ruin bars such as **Szimpla Kert** (p124) and clubs like Cuban **Havana** (p125).

DAY THREE
A Short Break

MORNING
Kickstart your morning by checking out fresh local produce, crafts and Hungarian specialities at **Nagycsarnok** (pictured; p133). Then walk along **Duna Korzó** (p81), admiring the city's pretty bridges.

AFTERNOON
Spend time exploring a treasure trove of history: the **National Museum** (p130), the **Great Synagogue** (p114; Europe's largest synagogue) and splendid **Basilica of St Stephen** (p92).

EVENING
Try local favourites at the bastion of Hungarian gastronomy, **Gundel** (p139), then enjoy a concert – at the Basilica, **Hungarian State Opera House** (p97) or **Liszt Music Academy** (p120) for elegant atmosphere, or at the **A38** (p60) decommissioned cargo ship for a laid-back experience.

If You Have More Time

Venture out to atmospheric Óbuda (p65) and visit the op-art **Victor Vasarely Museum** (p73), the idiosyncratic but delightful **Hungarian Museum of Trade and Hospitality** (p74) or the Roman ruins and museum of **Aquincum** (p68). Enjoy lunch at **Kéhli Vendéglő** (p75), which serves masterful Magyar meals in rustic surrounds.

Head up to the Buda Hills (p72) for a ride on the lovely **Children's Railway** (p69), then climb the **Elizabeth Lookout Tower** (p72) to reach Budapest's highest point. Try some Hungarian specialities such as *lángos* (deep-fried dough) or *rétes* (strudel) at **Normafa** (p72) before heading back to the city on the chairlift.

Catch Margaret Island's **musical fountain** (p105) after dark, then make your way to the city centre to a cool rooftop bar such as **360 Bar** (p125) or **St Andrea Skybar** (p85).

Elizabeth Lookout Tower (p72)

A City Day Trip

Though only 15 minutes from the city centre, **City Park** (p138) deserves a day of exploration. It's home to Budapest's most famous plaza, **Heroes' Square** (p138), world-renowned **Széchenyi Baths** (p139), the faux-historic but fairy-tale **Vajdahunyad Castle** (p138), the enormous **Budapest Zoo** (pictured; p140) and a handful of exquisite museums. Away from the big-ticket attractions are fun playgrounds, sports facilities, lovely cafes, cute dogs and plenty of green spaces. City Park hosted most of the events during Hungary's millenary celebrations back in 1896, while in recent years, the controversial Liget Budapest project has been undertaking renovations here.

On a Rainy Day

Budapest has amazing galleries and museums galore. The superstars are the **Museum of Fine Arts** (p138), **Hungarian National Gallery** (p39), **Castle Museum** (p37) and the **Hungarian National Museum** (p130). Quirkier stops include the **House of Terror** (p115), **Hospital in the Rock Nuclear Bunker Museum** (p42) and **Hungarian Museum of Trade and Hospitality** (p74).

———

Stay dry inside iconic houses of worship such as the **Basilica of St Stephen** (p92), **Great Synagogue** (pictured; p114) or **Rumbach Street Synagogue** (p117).

———

The interior of **Gellért Baths** (p52) is breathtaking, while settling in at a historic coffeehouse such as the **New York Café** (p120) is also delightful.

Get Prepared

BOOK AHEAD

Three months before
Book your accommodation and your ticket to sports events or big-name concerts or festivals such as **Sziget Festival** (p72).

One month before
Make reservations for must-see attractions and top-notch restaurants, and get familiar with the lingo.

One week before
Finalise your itinerary, buy your tickets for baths and public transport and check the weather forecast to pack accordingly.

Manners Matter

Punctuality is important. Arrive on time if you're invited somewhere or have a restaurant booking.

A firm but not-too-strong handshake is the most common greeting. For friends and family, it's two kisses on the cheek.

Say '*Egészségedre!*' (ay-gay-sheh-ged-reh), meaning 'to your health', when clinking glasses and make eye contact. Note that some Hungarians refuse to clink glasses of beer because this was how the Austrians celebrated the quelling of the 1848 Revolution.

Hungarikums

Hungary has Hungarikums – unique, culturally significant and nationally recognised products, practices or values that embody the essence of Hungarian heritage. These can include food and beverages, agricultural practices, folk art, traditions, inventions and even natural phenomena. Some examples are *lángos* (deep-fried dough), *pálinka* (fruit brandy), *gulyás* (goulash), Tokaj wines, Herend porcelain, teqball, the Rubik's cube and PICK salami. Some make lovely souvenirs to take home, while others you can try while in Budapest.

Things to Know

Budapest as we know it was born on 17 November 1873, when three cities officially merged into one. Buda is serene, hilly and historic; Pest is flat, lively and buzzing; and Óbuda is calm and quiet.

Knowing some thermal-bath etiquette comes in handy in the City of Spas. Bring swimwear, a towel, flip-flops (thongs) and swimming caps for doing laps. Shower and tie your hair back before entering the pools and keep the noise down. Bathing in thermal water isn't recommended for pregnant women and children under 14 – **Rudas** and **Veli Bej** baths won't even let kids enter.

Some museums and sights close on Mondays.

Service at shops and ticket offices can sometimes be slow and unfriendly. It's not personal and doesn't reflect on Hungarians in general.

TIPPING

Many restaurants automatically add a service charge of about 12% to the bill. If not included, tip the waiter by telling them how much you're paying in total.

10%
Restaurants & cafes

5-15%
Bars & pubs

Round up fare
Taxis for good service

Unusual
Hotel staff not necessarily expected

DAILY BUDGET

BUDGET: Less than 15,000Ft

- Dorm bed at a budget hostel: **from 3000Ft**
- Daily special or street food: **from 2000Ft**
- 24-hour public transport ticket: **2500Ft**
- Budget-friendly attractions: **from 1000Ft (some are free)**

MIDRANGE: 15,000-50,000Ft

- Three-star hotel or Airbnb: **from 10,000Ft**
- Meal at a midrange restaurant: **from 8000Ft**
- 72-hour public transport ticket: **5500Ft**
- Entry to popular attractions: **from 3000Ft**

TOP END: More than 50,000Ft

- Five-star hotel: **from 60,000Ft**
- Meal at a top-notch restaurant: **from 40,000Ft**
- Taxi ride: **from 4000Ft**
- Private tour: **from 10,000Ft**

Currency
Hungarian forint (HUF, Ft)

Language
Hungarian

Time
Central European Time (GMT/UTC +1)

SVETLANA SG/SHUTTERSTOCK ©

TIP

To save money, consider buying a Budapest Card which gives you free entry to a number of attractions, museums and thermal baths and comes with perks such as a cruise on the Danube.

When To Go

Budapest is always a good idea, holding something special in every season, from winter wonderlands and dreamy baths to buzzing garden clubs.

The capital is busiest in summer, when there's always something to do, from open-air film screenings to random bridge picnics and sipping *fröccs* (wine spritzers) on terraces, as well as during the winter holiday season when a festive spirit fills the city and Christmas markets appear on every corner. The shoulder seasons have pleasant weather, more reasonable prices and smaller crowds at museums and historic sites. In spring, Budapest is in full bloom, while autumn sees a riot of gorgeous reds, yellows and browns.

The Biggest Crowd Pleasers

June: Pride (p148) is Hungary's biggest LGBTIQ+ event, filling the capital with various events for several weeks. The festivities close with a well-attended colourful parade that brightens up the city's streets, leading to a rave Rainbow Party at Budapest Park.

August: The **Sziget Festival** (p72) takes place on an island within the city limits. The 'Island of Freedom' offers everything from big headliners to small local and international acts, circus shows, a travelling funfair and even bungee jumping.

September: Wooden kiosks set up around the Royal Palace serving the country's finest red, white and sparkling wines from various regions, as well as a plethora of foreign bottles, during the elegant **Budapest Wine Festival**.

December: Budapest's Christmas markets are among the best in Europe, with the main ones located

Budapest Weather

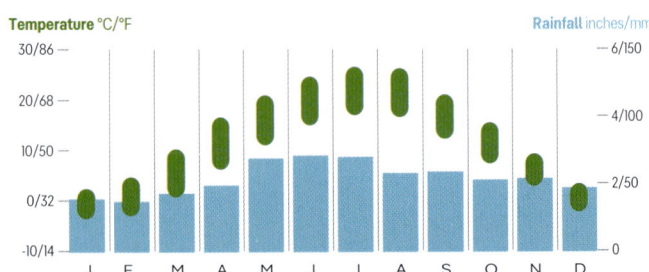

Budapest Pride (p148)

on **Vörösmarty tér** (p81) and in front of the **Basilica of St Stephen** (p92). They offer festive decor, handmade crafts and traditional Hungarian fare.

Cool & Quirky

May: **Budapest100** celebrates the city's architectural heritage. On this day, many notable buildings open their doors to the public for a sneak peek, tours and events.

May/June: To see *la vie en rosé* (life in rosé), head to **City Park** (p138) during the family-friendly **Rosalia Rosé and Champagne Festival**, offering refreshing rosés and fizzy champagnes.

June: On the closest weekend to the summer solstice, you can explore many of Budapest's museums after hours during **Night of Museums**. Special events, performances and guided tours generally take place.

August: Held at the **Royal Palace** (p36), the **Festival of Folk Arts** is Hungary's largest folk-art fair, with artisans from across the country and beyond showcasing their traditional crafts such as pottery, weaving and woodworking.

ACCOMMODATION LOWDOWN

Accommodation tends to be more expensive over summer and during the winter holidays, and big events push up prices too, so book well ahead if you're arriving for something specific. November, January and February offer the best bargains, but expect reduced or limited opening hours at major sights and attractions.

✈ Getting There

Budapest is the main point of entry for the majority of visitors to Hungary. Most people arrive by air, but you can also get here from cities throughout Europe by bus or train.

From the Airport to the City Centre

Airport Shuttle Bus (100E)

The **100E bus** provides a direct connection between the airport and the city centre, calling at Kálvin tér, Astoria and Deák Ferenc tér, which is a major transport hub at the heart of Budapest. It runs roughly every five to 10 minutes during the day, every 10 to 15 minutes in the early morning and every 30 to 40 minutes at night. It takes about 30 to 45 minutes, depending on traffic. Tickets cost 2200Ft and are available from ticket machines outside the airport or through the BudapestGO app.

Public Bus (200E)

The **200E bus** connects the airport to the Kőbánya-Kispest metro station, where you can transfer to metro line 3 (blue line) for the city centre. The metro stops at key locations such as Deák Ferenc tér, Nyugati pályaudvar and Ferenciek tere, running about every 10 minutes during the day and a little less frequently at night and in the morning. The journey takes about 40 to 60 minutes, and you need a regular public transport ticket to board.

Taxi

Walk outside the terminal to find the official taxi stand operated by **Főtaxi**, the airport's official taxi partner. Generally you only have to wait a couple of minutes. The ride typically takes 25 to 40 minutes and costs about 10,000 to 15,000 Ft.

Other Points of Entry

Train

The main international station is **Keleti** (p123), while other stations include **Nyugati** (p123) and **Déli**. All three are connected to metro lines of the same names; night buses serve them when the metro closes.

> **Bus**
> The main stations are **Népliget** and **Puskás Ferenc Stadion**. Both are on metro lines (M3 and M2 respectively) and are served by tram 1.

🚊 Getting Around

Budapest is a very walkable city, so if you're up for it, prepare for a great deal of wandering on foot. The public transport system is well-connected, frequent and reliable – trams, buses and four metro lines will get you everywhere you want to go. The bike- and e-scooter-sharing systems are great options, too.

Metro

Budapest has four underground metro lines (pictured below) that serve mostly the Pest side, but the red M2 line connects it to Buda. All metro lines run from about 4.30am to 11.30pm.

Tram

Trams are often fast and generally pleasant for sightseeing. Important tram lines include the scenic tram 2 (pictured right), which doubles as a sightseeing tour along the Pest side of the Danube. Opposite, on the Buda side, trams 19 and 41 do the same. The useful and frequent 4 and 6 start in south Buda and run the entire length of the Big Ring Rd in Pest before terminating at Széll Kálmán tér in Buda.

Bus

An extensive system of buses, with more than 270 routes day and night, serves greater Budapest. On certain lines, a bus may have an 'E' after its number, meaning it is express and makes limited stops. Services run from around 4.30am to between 9pm and 11.50pm,

FROM LEFT: SAVVAPANF PHOTO/SHUTTERSTOCK ©, XBRCHX/GETTY IMAGES ©

--- **ESSENTIAL APP** ---

Tickets and passes can be bought, stored and validated on the reliable **BudapestGO** app.

depending on the route. From 11.50pm to 4.30am, a network of night buses (beginning with 9) operates every 15 to 60 minutes, depending on the route.

HÉV

The HÉV suburban train line runs on five lines: north from Batthyány tér in Buda via Óbuda and Aquincum to Szentendre, south to both Csepel and Ráckeve, and east to Gödöllő. Lines are designated H5 to H9.

Taxi

Taxis are fully regulated and fairly priced by European standards. Reputable companies include Bolt, Fő Taxi, Uber and City Taxi. Don't hail cabs off the street and avoid the seemingly friendly touts waiting outside popular party destinations – call a reputable company instead. Taxis should have an identification badge displayed on the dashboard, as well as the logo of one of the reputable taxi firms displayed on the outside of the vehicle and a table of fares clearly visible on the window.

Bike Sharing

Download the **MOL Bubi** app to pick up/drop off bikes at any of the many green stations in Budapest, or the **Lime** app for e-scooters.

Public Transport Essentials

Tickets & Passes

BKK *(bkk.hu)* runs Budapest's public-transport network and has an integrated ticketing system. Tickets and daily or monthly passes are available from machines at stations or through the BudapestGO app and they enable you to board the city's metros, trams and buses. On the HÉV, regular tickets and passes are valid within city limits, but a separate ticket is needed for outside Budapest. Options range from single to 30-minute and 90-minute tickets or longer passes. If you buy a monthly pass, you'll need some form of identification, which you'll have to carry with you when using your pass. Note that children under six and people over 65 travel for free, while students with a valid EU student card get discounts.

Validating Tickets

Tickets do not only have to be purchased, but also validated. There are machines for paper tickets at metro stations and aboard trams and buses. Just stick your ticket in and it will be stamped. Digital tickets and passes come with a QR-code reader that you can use to scan QR codes displayed on machines at metro stations or on the sides of buses and trams. Just read the QR code until an animation pops up on your screen.

Controllers

Hungary has an old-fashioned way of ensuring everyone travels fairly. Armband-wearing controllers can appear anywhere, anytime, even at the bottom of the escalators before you exit the metro, so be sure to hold on to your validated tickets until the end of your journey. Note that some buses, especially on weekends, operate with front-door boarding only, in which case you must show your validated ticket to the driver.

TRAVEL COSTS

Single ticket
450Ft

Airport transfer ticket
2200Ft

MOL Bubi bike sharing
40Ft per minute

FARE EVASION

Getting caught without a valid ticket results in a 12,000Ft fine, paid on the spot or within two days.

TICKETS

Single ticket	450Ft
Collection of 10 tickets	4000Ft
30-minute ticket	530Ft
90-minute ticket	750Ft
24-hour ticket	2500Ft or 5000Ft for a group of up to five people
72-hour ticket	5500Ft
Half-monthly pass (15 days)	5950Ft
Monthly pass	8950Ft

TICKET ZONES

Budapest doesn't have travel zones. The public transport system covers the entire city in a single fare structure, meaning the same ticket or pass can be used across the capital, regardless of distance or area.

A Few Surprises

Unsettling scars from the past, hidden gems and unusual finds – if you look close enough, beautiful Budapest hides some surprising stuff.

Guerilla Statues

Hungarian-Ukrainian artist Mihály Kolodko deposits miniature masterpieces all around Budapest. The most famous include composer Franz Liszt sitting on his suitcase by the airport, Franz Joseph relaxing in a hammock on Liberty Bridge and Count Dracula reading a book behind Vajdahunyad Castle. They're not always easy to find, so our walking tour (p119) may come in handy.

Paternosters

Named after the opening words of 'Our Father' for their resemblance to a large rosary, paternosters are a rotating series of open cubicles that move continuously in a loop. You simply hop on when a cubicle reaches the floor level and then jump out on your desired floor. Though rare today, some government buildings, ministries and hospitals in Budapest still have them – one can be found inside a Brutalist office building on Thököly út 60, near City Park, though it's rarely turned on.

Bullet Holes

Some buildings are still dotted with bullet holes from the 1956 Uprising, when Hungarians revolted against communist rule. Some are original, such as those on the facade of the Hungarian National Archives and around the backstreets of district VIII, while others are re-creations, most famously on the arcades of the Ministry of Agriculture, commemorating 'Bloody Thursday', when the communists opened fire on a crowd of peaceful protesters, killing many.

Drinking Halls

Hungarians believe in the healing power of Budapest's mineral-rich thermal waters, which you can taste at the drinking halls of **Széchenyi**, **Rudas** and **Lukács** baths.

OFFBEAT BUDAPEST

A former secret nuclear bunker and hospital, the **Hospital in the Rock Nuclear Bunker Museum** even houses a helicopter. (p42)

Play around 150 vintage pinball machines at the quirky **Pinball Museum**. (p107)

Soak in a beer bath while serving yourself unlimited amounts of Czech beer at **Széchenyi Baths**. (p139)

Enjoy a fun Saturday drag show at **Alterego**, Budapest's top gay club. (p99)

Count Dracula sculpture by Mihály Kolodko (p119), City Park

Paternoster, Erzsébetváros

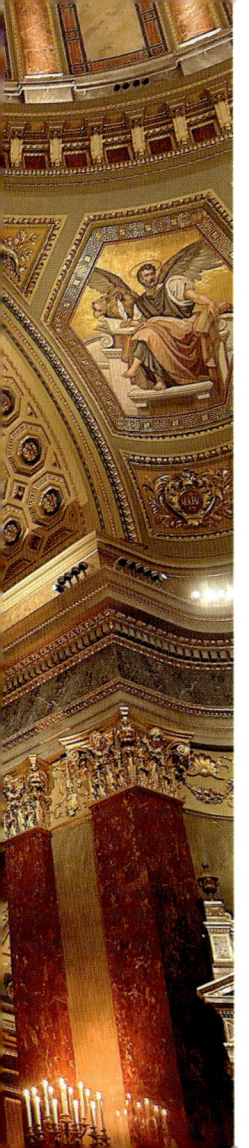

Explore Budapest

Castle District	33
Gellért Hill & Tabán	49
Óbuda & the Buda Hills	65
Belváros	77
Parliament & Around	87
Margaret Island & Northern Pest	101
Erzsébetváros & the Jewish Quarter	111
Southern Pest	127

Worth a Trip

Memento Park	62
City Park	138

Budapest's Walking Tours

Castle Hill	40
Gellért Hill & Tabán	56
The Buda Hills	70
Váci Utca & Vörösmarty Tér	80
The Triangle of Squares	94
The Length of Margaret Island	104
Erzsébetváros & the Jewish Quarter	116
Guerilla Statues	118
From Market to Market	132

Basilica of St Stephen (p92)
KATA FÁRI/LONELY PLANET ©

See p46 for eating, drinking and shopping listings

Explore
Castle District

Encompassing World Heritage–listed Castle Hill (Várhegy) and ground-level Víziváros, the Castle District is characterised by old-time charm, cobblestone streets and splendid staircases. With a magnificent monument on practically every corner, Várhegy is unparalleled for heavyweight sights crammed into a compact space: the Royal Palace, Fisherman's Bastion and Matthias Church are all steps from each other.

Víziváros offers fewer sights, but compensates with great restaurants, shops and pubs, especially around Széll Kálmán tér, the centre of urban Buda and the unofficial gateway to the Buda Hills.

At the time of writing, the district was undergoing major renovations as part of the National Hauszmann Alajos Program.

Getting Around

The easiest way to discover the neighbourhood is by walking, but wear comfy shoes for the cobblestone streets. There are various ways to reach Castle Hill.

 Bus 16
From Deák Ferenc tér in Pest, or Széll Kálmán tér in Buda.

 **Escalators/lifts**
From the Castle Garden Bazaar.

 **Funicular**
Arrive in style in the vintage cars of the funicular.

 **Walking**
Walk up on Várfok utca from Széll Kálmán tér, or on steeper stairs from Clark Ádám tér.

Matthias Church (p42)
KONOPLYTSKA/SHUTTERSTOCK ©

THE BEST

HISTORIC SIGHT Royal Palace (p36)

PHOTO OP Fisherman's Bastion (p42)

QUIRKY SIGHT Hospital in the Rock (p42)

VIEW Matthias Church's tower (p42)

MUSEUM Hungarian National Gallery (p39)

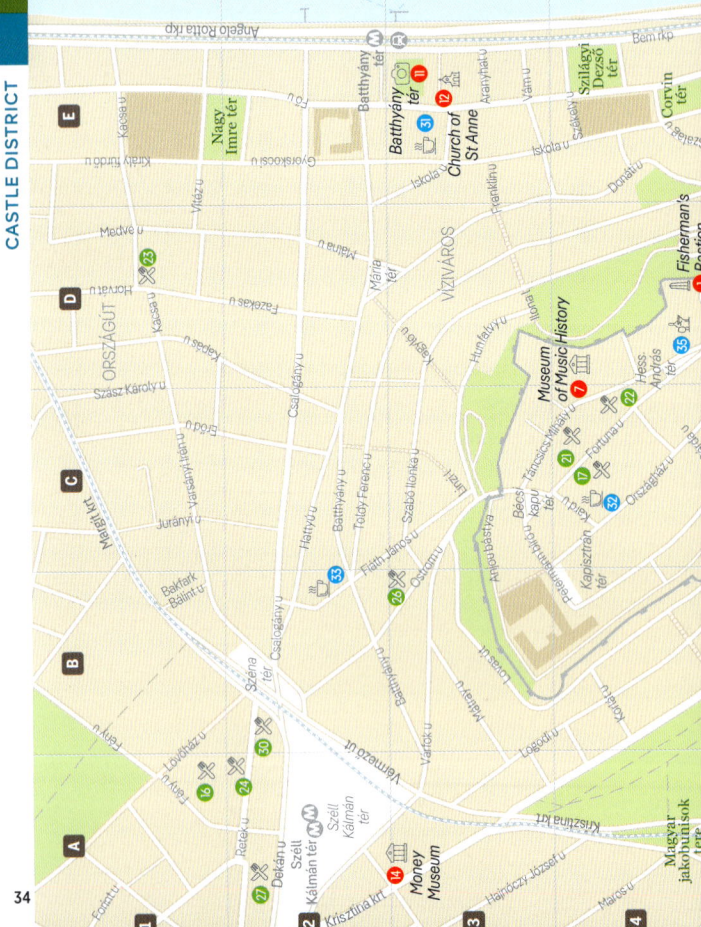

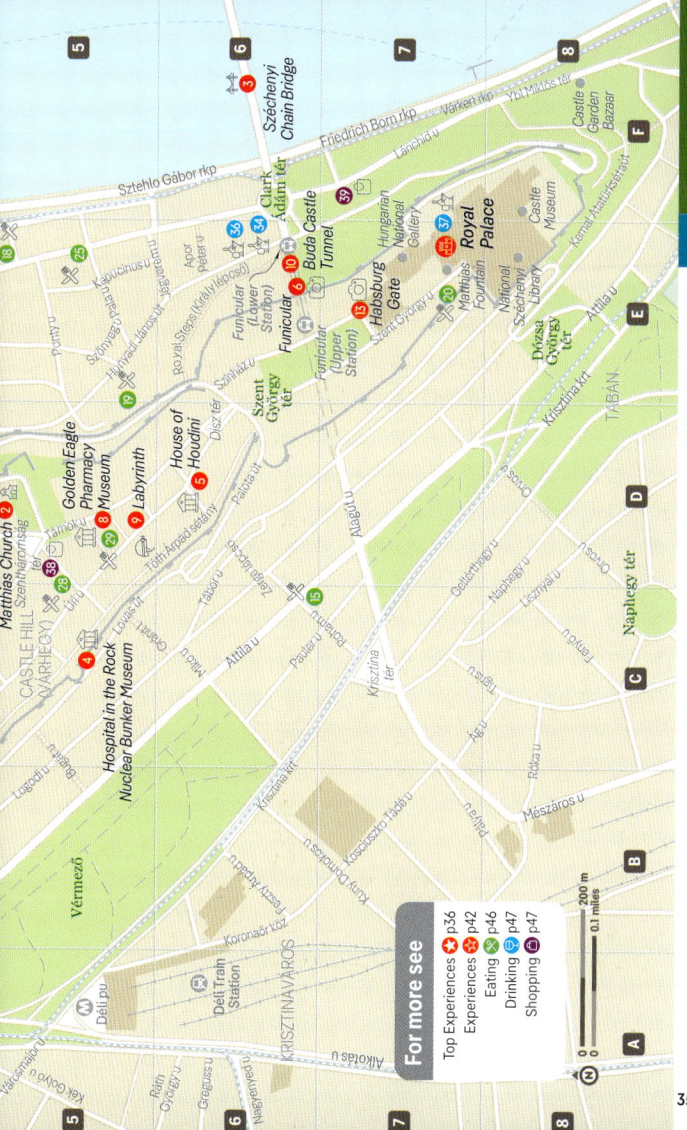

⭐ TOP EXPERIENCE

Royal Palace

Crowning Castle Hill, the emblematic Royal Palace is an architectural marvel with walls whispering tales of kings, wars and the undying spirit of a nation, as well as a cultural beacon that beckons travellers into the heart of Hungary's history, culture and literary and artistic legacy.

MAP P34 **F7**

The First Glimpse of Grandeur

A testament to Hungary's layered past, the Royal Palace was first built by King Béla IV, when he moved the county's capital from Esztergom to Buda in the mid-1200s, following the Mongol invasion that necessitated the construction of a fortified stronghold. Over the last seven centuries, it has been razed and rebuilt several times – in 1686, it was levelled in a war against the Turks, while during WWII it was bombed and robbed clean – and various architectural styles, from Gothic to Renaissance, Baroque and Neoclassical, have left their mark. Today, it houses the Hungarian National Gallery in buildings A through D, the Castle Museum in building E and the National Széchenyi Library in building F.

There are three ways to enter. It's best to head through the ornate, wrought-iron **Habsburg Gate** (p45) – surmounted by a bronze *turul* sculpture, the falcon-like totem of the Hungarians – and symmetrical stairways. You can also pass through the Corvinus Gate, topped by a black raven symbolising King Matthias Corvinus, or take the escalator, lift or steps from the **Castle Garden Bazaar** below the south end of Castle Hill.

Castle Museum

The **Castle Museum** retells the history of Budapest from prehistoric times to the present day. Discover restored rooms dating back to medieval times, statues of courtiers, squires and saints discovered during excavations in 1974, and the intriguing 'Light and Shadow:

PLANNING TIPS

Allow plenty of time at the Royal Palace if you plan to visit both museums. Arrive early in the morning to avoid crowds.

Scan this QR code for full opening hours and tickets.

ZGPHOTOGRAPHY/SHUTTERSTOCK ©

1000 Years of a Capital' exhibit that showcases the history of a city destroyed and rebuilt many times, taking a look at housing, ethnic diversity, religion and other issues over the centuries. For an extra charge, you can visit an absolute jewel box in this wing of the Royal Palace – St Stephen's Hall is a reconstructed 19th-century room filled with fine furnishings, the country's largest fireplace, wonderful ornaments and huge amounts of gold. Combined tickets are available.

National Széchenyi Library

The **National Széchenyi Library** contains codices and manuscripts, a large collection of foreign newspapers and a copy of everything published in Hungary or in the Hungarian language. It's also home to the largest state-of-the-art digitisation centre in Central Europe. Since it isn't a lending library, it allows members to do research, peruse the

QUICK BREAK
For something sweet, head to **Ruszwurm Cukrászda** (p47), Budapest's longest-standing pastry shop. For something more substantial in a historic setting, choose the **Royal Guard Restaurant & Cafe** (p46).

★ **TOP EXPERIENCE**

Hungarian National Gallery

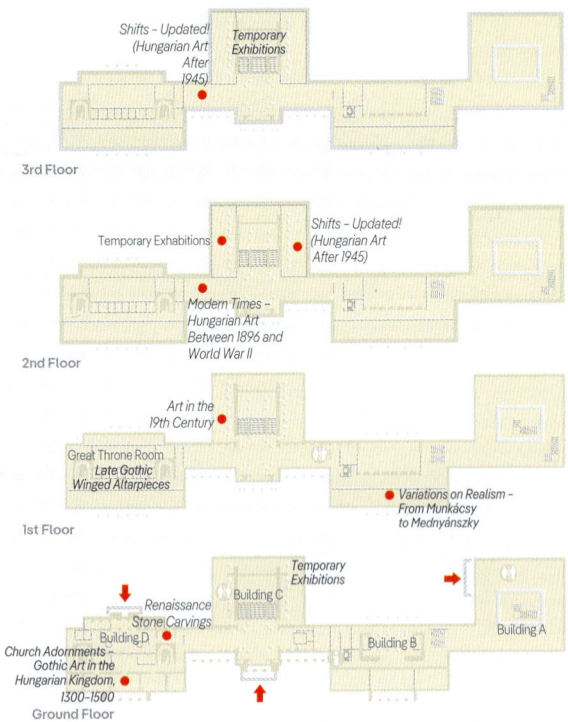

general stacks and read the large collection of foreign newspapers and magazines. A day pass is available.

Hungarian National Gallery

Comprising three wings and spread across four floors, the **Hungarian National Gallery** contains an overwhelming collection of thousands of artefacts presenting the rise of the fine arts in the country from the 11th century onwards. From the ground floor to the third floor, the permanent exhibitions present Renaissance stonework, Gothic church adornments, an important collection of paintings by the most prominent Hungarian artists of the 19th and 20th centuries, nude sculptures, late-Gothic winged altar pieces and a collection of international art from after 1800, as well as major temporary displays. The third floor also provides access to the palace's dome for breathtaking views.

Matthias Fountain

Nicknamed Hungary's Trevi Fountain, **Matthias Fountain**, in the Hunyadi Courtyard next to the Hungarian National Gallery, is a popular sight. It was designed by famed fin-de-siècle sculptor Alajos Stróbl in 1904 and completely rebuilt with the help of his grandson, Mátyás Stróbl, in 2020. The central figure portrays one of the most popular Hungarian monarchs, King Matthias the Just, in hunting attire, resting after killing a deer stag. To his right is Szép Ilonka (Beautiful Helena) cradling a deer. In Mihály Vörösmarty's famous poem, Szép Ilonka falls in love with a dashing young hunter – the king in disguise – and, on learning his identity and feeling unworthy of his love, dies of a broken heart. Note that the middle one of the king's dogs looks slightly different to the other two. This is because it was blown up in WWII and, though it was quickly replaced, the quality differs. Below the fountain lies the family crypt of the Habsburgs, accessible from the Hungarian National Gallery on guided tours.

MAGYAR MASTERPIECES
At the Hungarian National Gallery, look for the works of Mihály Munkácsy, the 'painter of the Great Plain', Pál Szinyei Merse, Hungary's foremost Impressionist, and Tivadar Kosztka Csontváry.

TIVADAR KOSZTKA CSONTVÁRY
Though he only picked up painting when he was 41, never sold a painting in his life and died penniless, many critics consider Csontváry Hungary's greatest painter.

Walk Castle Hill

There's no better introduction to Budapest than a walk around Castle Hill. The neighbourhood has everything that defines this delightful city: history, architecture, fabulous views and tourists in spades. If you'd like to take in the first three but avoid the last, make this an early morning walk.

START	END	LENGTH
Széll Kálmán tér	Royal Riding Hall	2km; two hours

1 A Medieval Entrance

Start from Széll Kálmán tér and walk up Várfok utca to the **Vienna Gate**, the old town's medieval entrance. Climb to the top for orientating views of the old town. The pretty building with the mesmerising maiolica-tiled roof to the west is the National Archives.

2 An Old-timey Street

Táncsics Mihály utca is full of little houses painted in lively hues and adorned with statues. At No 26, you'll find the **Medieval Jewish Prayer House** – a place of worship and exhibition hall in one. No 7 is home to the **Museum of Music History** (p44), while No 9 is a **former political prison** where two figures of the 1848–49 Freedom Fights, Lajos Kossuth and Mihály Táncsics, were famously jailed.

3 Awesome Views

Keep going straight until you reach Szentháromság tér – on your way you'll pass the architecturally controversial Hilton Budapest, topped with the great rooftop **White Raven** bar (p47). Lace-like **Matthias Church** (p42) towers above the square, while the white, 140m-long neo-Gothic **Fisherman's Bastion** (p42) offers one of the best views of the Pest skyline, and excellent photo ops.

4 Coffee & Cake

Turn onto Szentháromság utca to reach family-run **Ruszwurm Cukrászda** (p47), Budapest's oldest pastry shop. **Herend** (p47) next door sells delicate, handcrafted and world-famous Hungarian porcelain.

5 Magic & Mysteries

Colourful and quiet Úri utca is home to the **Labyrinth** (p44) at No 9. Walk further south to find the **House of Houdini** (p43) on the right-hand side, then keep going straight.

6 Home of Hungary's President

As you walk, you'll pass the former **Carmelite Monastery** on the left, now home to the office of Hungary's prime minister. **Sándor Palace** is the official office and residence of the country's president. A rather low-key but ceremonial changing of the guard takes place hourly.

7 A Vintage Ride

In front of Sándor Palace is the upper station of the **funicular** (p43), which will take you down to Clark Ádám tér in cute vintage carriages. From here, you'll see the **Habsburg Gate** (p45), an ornate entrance to the Royal Palace grounds topped by a *turul* statue.

8 More Great Photo Ops

Wander around the castle grounds, then head behind the Royal Palace to see the renovated neo-Renaissance **Stöckl Steps** connecting the Castle Garden with the pretty **Royal Riding Hall**, which is today an events space.

EXPERIENCES

Snap Photos at Fisherman's Bastion VIEWPOINT
MAP: ❶ P34 D4

The 140m-long neo-Gothic **Fisherman's Bastion** *(fishermans bastion.com)* offers one of the prettiest panoramas over the Pest skyline. The bastion is a faux historic monument, built as a viewpoint in 1905 by famed architect Frigyes Schulek to offset nearby Matthias Church. Its name comes from the medieval guild of fishermen responsible for defending this stretch of the old castle wall. The seven cone-topped turrets represent the seven Magyar chieftains who settled in this part of the Carpathian Basin in the late 9th century. The upstairs viewing platform requires a ticket *(adult/student 1200/600Ft)*.

Marvel at Matthias Church CHURCH
MAP: ❷ P34 D5

With a lace-like facade and a roof covered in colourful Zsolnay tiles, neo-Gothic **Matthias Church** *(matyas-templom.hu; adult/student 2900/2300Ft)* has changed many times over the course of the last millennium. What you see today is something akin to the Gothic landmark that stood here in the 13th century – this is thanks to Frigyes Schulek, who went back to the original medieval plans when redesigning the church in the late 19th century. A great way to see the cathedral's interior is to attend one of the many classical concerts held inside. The star is the organ. For stunning views, climb the tower.

Walk Across Chain Bridge BRIDGE
MAP: ❸ P34 F6

Arguably the city's most striking span, the **Széchenyi Chain Bridge** – built between 1840 and 1849 – was the first permanent bridge between Buda and Pest. Its name honours its initiator, the great Hungarian statesman Count István Széchenyi, and was built by Scotsman Adam Clark. When crossing the bridge, get the world's smallest violin out for all the noblemen who, though previously exempt from taxation, had to pay a toll just like everyone else in order to cross. Luckily for them, the toll was lifted in 1918. The Chain Bridge is particularly beautiful lit up at night. The lighting gets special colours on national holidays and anniversaries.

Tour the Hospital in the Rock UNDERGROUND MUSEUM
MAP: ❹ P34 C5

Part of the Castle Hill cave network, the **Hospital in the Rock Nuclear Bunker Museum** *(sziklakorhaz.eu; adult/child 9500/4800Ft)* is an underground hospital that was turned into a nuclear bunker kept secret for decades – the government only declassified its existence in 2002. Many patients were treated here during WWII and the 1956 Uprising. It includes a maze of wards full of mysteries and untold stories, as well as some 200 lifelike wax figures, original furniture and medical equipment from the 1940s and '50s – and even a helicopter. You can visit through a one-hour guided tour that departs hourly between 10am and 6pm.

Get Impressed by the House of Houdini MUSEUM

MAP: ❺ P34 D6

The **House of Houdini** (houseof houdinibudapest.com; adult/child 5200/3200Ft) honours one of history's greatest illusionists, Harry Houdini, who was born Erik Weisz in Budapest. Enter the museum after solving a playful puzzle, then admire a vast collection of original items from Houdini's life, including personal letters and century-old handcuffs. At the end of the visit, you'll be treated to a short live-magic performance.

Ride the Funicular FUNICULAR

MAP: ❻ P34 E6

The steep, 95m-long track of the **funicular** (siklojegy.hu; adult/child 5000/2000Ft) offers a quick and convenient way up to the **Royal Palace** (p36) from the banks of the Danube, climbing at a speed of 1.5m per second and providing splendid views en route. Opened in 1870, it was only the second funicular in the world – eight years after the first in Lyon, France – and was originally powered by a steam engine. In 1944, the structure was severely damaged during the war. Although there were several propositions to carry out renovations, it wasn't until 1986 that it finally reopened to the public. To mark its 150th anniversary in 2020, all of the rails along the track were replaced and the two little carriages, named *Margit* and *Gellért*, were overhauled with vintage-looking wooden fittings. Buy your ticket online to avoid queuing.

 WHO'S GOT THE CATS' TONGUES?

The dearly loved lion sculptures on Chain Bridge are the protagonists of many an urban legend. According to one, when a young apprentice pointed out that the lions all lacked tongues, the Hungarian sculptor, proud of his new creations, jumped off the bridge into the Danube. While the story's credibility is highly questionable, the lions have divided people for decades – some see tongues, others don't – and watchful eyes will spot many a curious soul peeking into their mouths. So, do they have tongues? We recommend you take a look yourself.

Play at the Museum of Music History
MUSEUM

MAP: ❼ P34 C4

Housed in an 18th-century palace with a lovely courtyard, the **Museum of Music History** *(zti.hu; adult/student 2000/1000Ft)* might be small, but it has a lot to offer. Peruse the instruments, piano rolls and music-themed works of art to learn about the development of music in Hungary from the 18th century to the present day. See magnificent musical instruments made by Hungarian craftsmen from the 18th century onwards, such as an organ, pedal harp, square piano and typically Hungarian instruments like the cimbalom (dulcimers), as well as paintings and medals depicting famous Hungarian composers such as Liszt, Erkel, Bartók and Kodály.

Visit the Golden Eagle Pharmacy
MUSEUM

MAP: ❽ P34 D5

Discover a mock-up of an alchemist's laboratory with creepy stuffed creatures and a rack of herbs at the **Golden Eagle Pharmacy Museum** *(semmelweismuseum.hu/arany-sas-patikamuzeum; adult/child 1000/500Ft)*. It's located on the site of Budapest's first pharmacy, which was in operation until WWI.

Descend into the Labyrinth
CAVE MUSEUM

MAP: ❾ P34 D5

A macabre site, the **Labyrinth** *(labirintus.eu; adult/child 5000/1000Ft)* guards legends and ghost stories that continue to haunt the castle caves. Expect ruins dating back to the Middle Ages, cave paintings (reproductions), coffins, a motley collection of wax figures and the chamber of the Labyrinth's most notorious resident, Dracula – the Wallachian prince, Vlad Tepes, also known as Vlad the Impaler, was the real-life inspiration for Bram Stoker's seminal antihero. There's also a stretch where you can experience complete darkness with only your other senses and mysterious music to guide you for about five minutes.

Climb Atop the Buda Castle Tunnel
TUNNEL

MAP: ❿ P34 E6

With Castle Hill standing at the Buda end of the Chain Bridge, it was decided to carve a **tunnel** into the hill to ease traffic. This took just eight months in 1853, with the limestone providing few challenges. Note the windows on its facade, which used to belong to an actual apartment that was home to the Chain Bridge's caretaker for decades. While you should avoid walking through the tunnel to protect your lungs, climbing on top of it presents a great photo opportunity. Between the tunnel and the bridge, the flower-strewn roundabout named after Adam Clark is where the Víziváros neighbourhood begins. Local lore has it that when it rains, Chain Bridge is pulled into the tunnel to protect its revered stone lions.

Snap Perfect Pics on Batthyány Tér
SQUARE

Batthyány tér (MAP: ⑪ P34 **E3**) is the centre of Víziváros and the best place to take pictures of the majestic Parliament building across the Danube. The square is home to an imposing market hall full of fresh, colourful produce, as well as one of Budapest's prettiest Baroque churches, the twin-towered, 18th-century **Church of St Anne** (MAP: ⑫ P34 **E3**).

Batthyány tér is an important transport hub – you can catch the M2 metro to Pest or Széll Kálmán tér, as well as the H5 HÉV suburban train line to splendid Szentendre, from here (Budapest's Óbuda neighbourhood is on the way).

Pass Through the Ornate Habsburg Gate
GATE

MAP: ⑬ P34 **E7**

Habsburg Gate provides a magnificent entrance to the Royal Palace's sprawling front terrace, with its Baroque styling and elaborate wrought-iron lampposts creating a statuesque welcome for visitors. The dual stairways are symmetrical, and the eastern flight is a great place to snap a photo of the Pest skyline. You can't miss the 1905 bronze *turul* statue – a falcon-like totem of the ancient Magyars and a national symbol – clinging onto the gate with its wings outstretched and a sword in its talons.

Enjoy the Money Museum
MUSEUM

MAP: ⑭ P34 **A3**

Housed in an incredible, eclectic Secessionist building, the **Money Museum** *(penzmuzeum.hu; admission free)* extends over three floors and is based on interactivity and individual experience while focusing on all things money, money, money. Tip: the museum cafe is on the rooftop terrace, right next to an ornate turret. Booking your museum visit ahead is necessary.

 THE LEGEND OF THE TURUL

The mythic, falcon-like *turul* is the national symbol of Hungary and first appeared in a 9th-century legend, *Emese's Dream*. In the story, the pregnant Emese saw the *turul* in a dream, during which the bird revealed that Emese would give birth to a line of mighty rulers. Her son, Álmos, became one of the seven chieftains who led their peoples to the Carpathian Basin. His son, Árpád, was the greatest ruler of the Magyar tribes, beginning a three-century-long dynasty of kings. Recently, groups with far-right ideologies have been using the *turul* as their symbol.

LISTINGS

Best Places for...

❸ Budget **❸❸** Midrange **❸❸❸** Top End

Eating

Hungarian Favourites

Stand25 ❸❸
15 C6
Traditional Hungarian classics with a Mediterranean edge by Bocuse d'Or Europe winner Tamás Széll. *noon-4pm & 5.30pm-midnight Mon-Sat*

Fény utca Market ❸
16 A1
Market hall offering fresh local produce, organic goods and various stalls serving quick but filling bites and street food. *hours vary*

Pierrot ❸❸
17 C4
A sophisticated Hungarian restaurant in a 13th-century building. The lovely garden is a delight. *11.30am-11pm Wed-Sun*

Horgásztanya Vendéglő ❸❸
18 E5
Freshwater-fish soup is served in bowls, pots or kettles, and your carp, catfish or trout might be prepared Baja, Tisza-or spicy Szeged style. A must try. *noon-11pm*

With Views

Aranybástya ❸❸❸
19 E5
A 'Hungarikum' menu introduces you to the country's time-honoured recipes; the views from the terrace are breathtaking. *noon-10pm*

Royal Guard Restaurant & Cafe ❸❸
20 E7
A lovely cafe-cum-restaurant inside the renovated 1903 building of the Royal Guard, overlooking Matthias Fountain and the Royal Palace. *11am-9.30pm*

The Feeling of Home

21 Magyar Vendéglő ❸❸
21 C4
Homestyle Hungarian dishes with a modern twist and an impressive assortment of local wines. *noon-11.45pm*

Pest-Buda ❸❸
22 C4
Hungarian meals just like a Magyar grandmother would make, inside a boutique hotel. *7.30am-10pm*

See p34 for map of locations

Mandragóra ❸❸
23 D1
This family-run restaurant has earned loyal local fans over the past 20 years for its excellent takes on Hungarian classics. *11.30am-10.30pm Mon-Sat*

International Fare

Giulia ❸❸
24 A2
An 'under promise, over deliver' modern trattoria offering the best of Italian cuisine. *4-11pm Tue-Fri, noon-11pm Sat & Sun*

Pavillon de Paris ❸❸
25 E5
Imaginative French cuisine and excellent service. During the warmer months, head to the lovely garden. *noon-11pm*

Arany Kaviár ❸❸❸
26 B3
Luxury, prestige and lots of caviar. For a bespoke culinary experience presented by chef José Guerrero, book the World Table experience. *6pm-midnight Tue-Sat*

Pingrumba ❸❸
27 A2
At this cool restaurant, the culinary journey

takes you from Cairo to Calcutta. *5–11pm Mon-Wed, noon–midnight Thu-Sat, noon–10pm Sun*

Sweet Spots

Ruszwurm Cukrászda €€€
 C5

Dating back to 1827, this is the longest-operating pastry shop in Budapest, with one of the city's best *krémes* (a kind of vanilla custard cake). *10am–7pm summer, to 6pm winter*

Budavári Rétesvár €€
 D5

Excellent Hungarian strudel *(rétes)* with various fillings, savoury snacks and lovely coffees and teas. *8am–8pm*

Á Table €
 B2

Branch of a popular bakery chain that charms Budapest with excellent pastries, Danishes, savoury snacks and coffee. *7am–6pm Mon-Fri, 8am–5pm Sat & Sun*

Drinking

Cute Cafes

Steamhouse Cafe
 E3

Coffee with a view on the top floor of a market overlooking the Danube and Parliament. Excellent blends and tasty pastries. *8am–6pm Mon-Fri, 9am–3pm Sat*

4 perc és kávé
 C4

Perfect for a quick coffee stop, this bite-sized cafe is fully vegan, making java mostly from oat milk. *8.30am–6pm Mon-Fri, 9am–6pm Sat & Sun*

Bereg Embassy Bar & Cafe
 B2

Located in a remarkable example of Hungarian 'organic architecture', this place welcomes 'wanderers, lovers, artists' and more. There's a peaceful garden. *11.30am–11pm Mon-Sat*

Bars & Pubs

Leo Budapest
 E6

Atop Hotel Clark, Leo Budapest offers an urban-jungle atmosphere and a close-up view of Chain Bridge, the winding river and the Royal Palace. *noon–midnight*

White Raven
D4

You can see pretty much all of Budapest from White Raven, including a unique perspective on the intricate roof of Matthias Church. *noon–10pm*

Lánchíd Söröző
 E6

A wonderful retro Magyar feel amid old movie posters, red-checked tablecloths and classic rock through the speakers. A proper local place with friendly service. *noon–11pm*

Savoyai Terasz
 E7

Delicious coffee and dazzling views at the foot of the Royal Palace, plus plenty of music events, especially in summer. *10.30am–8pm*

Shopping

Take Something Home

Herend
D5

For fine porcelain, there's no other place to go. Delicate, handcrafted Herend porcelain pieces are world famous and a Hungarikum (p20). *10am–6pm Mon-Fri, to 2pm Sat*

Bortársaság
F7

An exceptional selection of Hungarian wines by the bottle – no one knows home-grown wines like these guys. *11am–8pm Mon-Fri, to 7pm Sat*

Explore
Gellért Hill & Tabán

Tree-dotted Gellért Hill, surmounted by the Citadel and the Liberty Monument, is one of Budapest's signature landmarks. From the top, the views are unbeatable, while below, Szent Gellért tér is an important transport hub and home to captivating Gellért Baths.

Tabán is the leafy and hilly neighbourhood stretching between Gellért Hill and Castle Hill. Once Budapest's Montmartre, it was a bohemian district that is now one of the capital's calmest and quietest neighbourhoods – it's mostly a huge green park with more picnic spots and playgrounds than sights, safeguarding its village-like atmosphere in legend and memory only. On the other side of Gellért Hill, hip Bartók Béla út is the happening part of otherwise sleepy south Buda.

Getting Around

 M4 Metro
Take the M4 to reach Pest or Kelenföld station, from where buses head to Memento Park.

 Trams 47 & 49
Both trams travel to south Buda, or across Liberty Bridge to Pest.

 Trams 19 & 41
These trams follow the Danube on the Buda side, and can take you as far as Óbuda.

 Bus 27
Hop on this bus to avoid the steep climb up Gellért Hill.

THE BEST

VIEWPOINT Gellért Hill (p54)

HISTORIC MONUMENT Liberty Monument (p54)

HISTORIC SPA Gellért Baths (p52)

CONCERT VENUE A38 (p60)

ADRENALINE SPIKE RedJet (p58)

Liberty Monument (p54)
LOSTINTHECITY/SHUTTERSTOCK ©

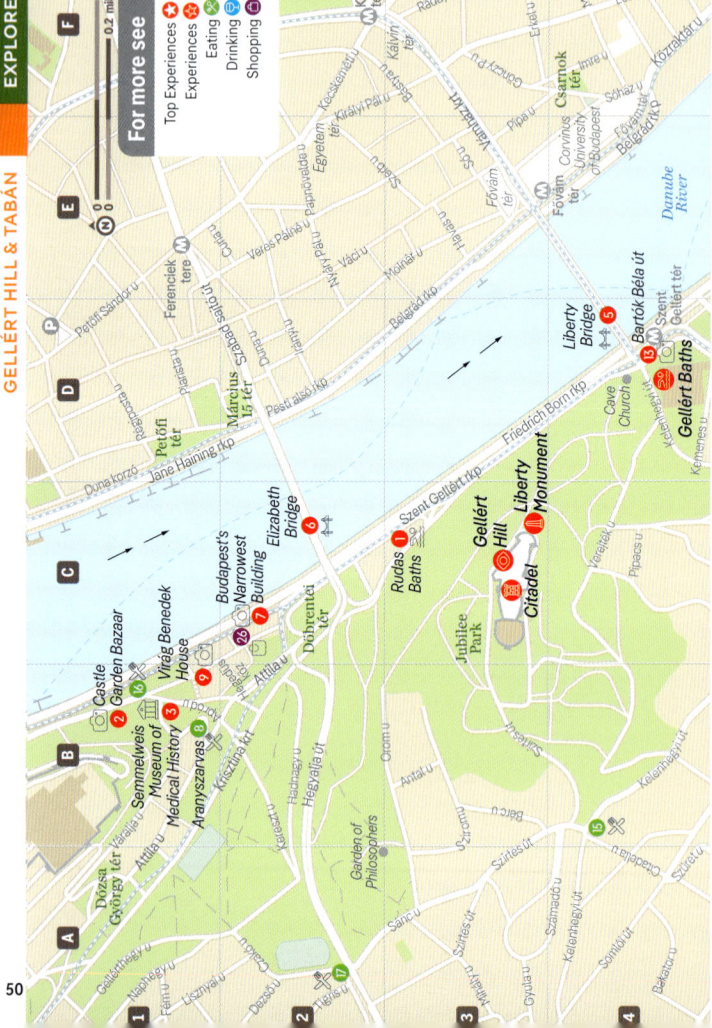

EXPLORE

GELLÉRT HILL & TABÁN

51

★ **TOP EXPERIENCE**

Gellért Baths

An Art Nouveau masterpiece, Gellért Baths, at the foot of Gellért Hill, is unquestionably one of Budapest's most stunning historic spas. Its swimming pool is the prettiest in town and its thermal pools are full of mineral-rich healing hot waters.

MAP: P50 **D4**

PLANNING TIPS
Arrive early and on a weekday to avoid crowds. There's a restaurant and cafe inside. Swimming caps are compulsory in the swimming pool.

Scan this QR code for opening hours and tickets.

History

The origins of Gellért Baths can be traced to ancient times, with the first written chronicle about them dating to the 10th century. It became a beloved bathing spot during the Turkish occupation in the 15th century. In the 17th century, locals referred to them as the Sáros-fürdő (Mud Baths) due to the presence of fine mud that settled at the pool's bottom and mixed with the spring water. The Mud Baths had to be demolished when the predecessor to today's Liberty Bridge was being built. Gellért Baths opened on 26 September 1918, setting a new standard of opulence in the city. Expansions added fun features such as a wave pool in 1927, and later a whirlpool.

Healing Hot Water

The richly embellished interior makes bathing in the hot waters feel like a royal ritual. The thermal pools range in temperature from 35°C to 40°C, and there's a cooler pool for swimming laps. The water emanates from deep within Gellért Hill and is rich in sodium, calcium and magnesium, among other minerals. These are fortifying against a number of ailments, from circulation-related disorders and spine and vertebrae injuries to degenerative illnesses and joint problems. Except for the cold plunge pools, all pools contain thermal

POSZTOS/SHUTTERSTOCK ©

water in full or diluted quantities. An outside thermal pool overlooks the Buda Hills, and a fun wave pool entertains crowds of all ages in summer. Other amenities include medical massages, a sauna, steam cabin and drinking fountains.

Just The Two of Us

If you're after a more intimate experience, you can enjoy a private 90-minute bathing session. You'll get a room adorned with Zsolnay porcelain tiles and a special marble tub all to yourself, as well as access to a hot-air chamber for relaxation. A bottle of champagne and chocolate desserts are included. Booking in advance is a must.

QUICK BREAK
Trendy Bartók Béla út is just around the corner, with several eating and drinking options, including the lovely **Kelet Café & Gallery** (p61).

⭐ TOP EXPERIENCE

Gellért Hill & Liberty Monument

One of Budapest's iconic landmarks, tree-dotted Gellért Hill is topped with two emblematic symbols of the city: the Citadel and the Liberty Monument. Climb the 235m-high peak for amazing views of Buda, the Pest skyline, the bridges and the river, and to find playgrounds and a slide park.

MAP: P50 **C3**

PLANNING TIPS
To reach the top, start from Elizabeth Bridge and head towards the statue of St Gellért, choose a less steep but slightly longer journey from Liberty Bridge, or hop on bus 27. Climb Gellért Hill at dawn for a spectacular sunrise.

Scan this QR code for more information.

Citadel & Liberty Monument

While other such fortresses were generally built for defence, Budapest's **Citadel** was erected after the 1848–49 Revolution – when Hungary wanted to break from Habsburg rule – to discourage further insurrections. Big guns were aimed at the city from holes dotting the outside walls. Today, Hungarians think of the Citadel not as a symbol of repression, but one of freedom. This sentiment is reinforced by the lovely lady – the **Liberty Monument** – with a palm frond in her outstretched arms. Inaugurated in 1947, the 40m-high statue originally aimed to honour the Soviet soldiers who died 'liberating' Budapest in 1945, but after the regime change, the statues of the soldiers were sent to Memento Park (p62) and the monument now commemorates everyone who sacrificed their lives for Hungary's freedom. At the time of writing, the Citadel was closed for renovations and was set to reopen as a public park with viewpoints and an exhibition space in late 2025.

Cave Church

On the walk up Gellért Hill, peek into the functioning **Cave Church** (*sziklatemplom.hu; adult/student 1200/1000Ft*). This naturally formed grotto was turned into a church in 1931 and expanded outward into a neo-Romanesque monastery three years later. The church served as the seat of Hungary's Pauline

St Gellért statue, Gellért Hill
JENNIFER WALKER/SHUTTERSTOCK ©

order (the only male religious order founded in the country) until 1951, when the communists imprisoned the priests and the cave was sealed off with a thick concrete wall, part of which is still visible today as a reminder. The Pauline monks eventually returned after the fall of communism. The church can be visited anytime except during Mass; the interior remains a constant 20°C year-round, with no heating required.

Garden of Philosophers

Most people who come to Gellért Hill head straight up to the Citadel for the postcard panoramas, but if you prefer quiet rumination to the buzz of crowds, consider a detour to the **Garden of Philosophers** on the hillside closer to Elizabeth Bridge.

QUICK BREAK
Búsuló Juhász (p61) on Gellért Hill is a lovely restaurant with superb dishes and a serene view.

WALKING TOUR

Walk Gellért Hill & Tabán

This scenic walk takes you to lush parks, historic landmarks and awe-inspiring viewpoints, revealing Budapest's vibrant past and natural beauty while providing excellent photo opportunities. From hearty food to a pulse-raising route, with soaks in healing waters for reward, this tour has everything you need.

START	END	LENGTH
ODA	Bartók Béla út	3.5km; two to three hours

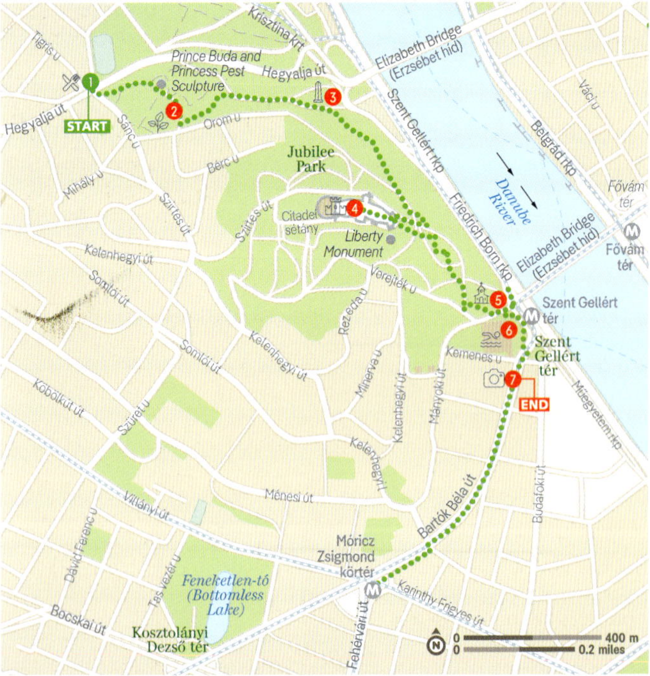

1 Begin with Breakfast

Start your morning with a big, energising breakfast at **ODA** (p61), housing three different restaurants inside the oldest house in Tabán. You'll find everything from morning pick-me-ups to pizza, Hungarian dishes and even bao buns. Then head up Gellért Hill towards the Garden of Philosophers.

2 Peace & Views

The **Garden of Philosophers** (p55) is a green space filled with bronze statues of eight famous thinkers and prophets from all over the world, including Jesus Christ, Buddha, Akhenaten and Mahatma Gandhi. The lovely sculpture depicting the union of Prince Buda and Princess Pest is a delight. It's a perfect place for some quiet pondering and to enjoy the dazzling view to the Royal Palace and the Pest side.

3 A Pulse-raising Walk

Keep walking on Gellért Hill and head to the **Statue of St Gellért** to enjoy a panorama of the gleaming-white Elizabeth Bridge and its surroundings, as well as a summer-only waterfall below the statue. Then follow the steps leading all the way to the Citadel.

4 Rewarding Views

The area around the **Citadel** (p54) is perfect for photography, since it provides one of the prettiest panoramas of Budapest, the Danube and its bridges, as well as a close-up view of the iconic **Liberty Monument** (p54). By late 2025, the Citadel is set to turn into a huge public park and events and exhibition space, and the Liberty Monument will be renovated.

5 A Church in a Cave

After you've looked around and snapped enough pics, start heading down the hill on the other side by taking the stairs in front of the Liberty Monument. The fascinating **Cave Church** (p54) is carved into the hillside before you reach the bottom.

6 Spa Break

One you reach the bottom of the hill, the entrance to magnificent **Gellért Baths** (p52) will be right in front of you. Plunging into the muscle-melting, mineral-rich thermal pools within the astonishing Art Nouveau interior is just what you'll need after the walk.

7 Mingle with Locals

Once you're ready to leave the baths, head to **Bartók Béla út** (p60) for food and drinks. This street is the happening part of Buda, full of cool restaurants and bars side-by-side, catering mostly to a hip local crowd and offering everything from vegan street food to local favourites and wine.

EXPERIENCES

Soak at Rudas Baths
BATHHOUSE

MAP: ① P50 C3

At historic **Rudas Baths** *(rudas furdo.hu; entry 9300-13200Ft),* contemporary design elements mix with centuries-old bathhouse features. The star attraction is the rooftop hot tub, providing a grand view of the entire Pest skyline. Rudas is Budapest's only bathhouse that retains single-sex days on weekdays and welcomes night owls on weekends. There's also an ornate drinking hall, where visitors can sample some of the mineral-rich liquid. No under-14s.

Tour the Castle Garden Bazaar
PLEASURE PARK

MAP: ② P50 B1

History meets the present day at this stunning neo-Renaissance complex, which overlooks the Buda riverfront at the foot of the Royal Palace. Today, the **Castle Garden Bazaar** *(varkertbazar. hu)* serves as a cultural hub with ample space for a variety of events: concerts, open-air film screenings and exhibitions. Stairs, lifts and an escalator make getting up to the Royal Palace from the Garden Bazaar easy. Opposite, the elegant **Felix Kitchen & Bar** (p61) is housed inside a beautiful building that once pumped water to the Royal Palace.

Get Familiar with Medical History
MUSEUM

MAP: ③ P50 B1

The house on Apród utca where Ignác Semmelweis was born and buried is today home to the partly quirky, partly grisly and partly moving **Semmelweis Museum of Medical History** *(semmelweismuseum.hu; adult/ student 1400/700Ft),* presenting the history of medicine, beginning with ancient Egypt, as well as a section dedicated to the life and work of Semmelweis. The 'saviour of mothers' discovered the cause of puerperal (childbirth) fever, but spent the rest of his life mocked, ridiculed and subsequently committed to an insane asylum, where he died at the age of 47. Decades later, his achievements were validated, and Semmelweis is now globally recognised. Expect a gorgeous pharmacy from 1813, the world's first surgical stapler designed and used by Hümer Hültl and a unique model of a dentist's office and laboratory.

Get Your Adrenaline Pumping
SPEEDBOAT

MAP: ④ P50 F8

For a hair-raising ride, book yourself a seat on **RedJet** *(redjet.hu; 13,500Ft)* and buckle up. This 12-seat speedboat zooms by Budapest's most splendid sights on 30-minute trips, its 440HP engine propelling it along at 80km/h. RedJet performs stunts on the way: stopping, restarting and spinning in front of and under historic landmarks such as the Parliament and Chain Bridge. Catch RedJet at BudaPart Kopaszigát, a car- and dog-free sandy riverside recreational zone full of restaurants, ice-cream parlours, cafes and bars in south Buda.

Cross Historic Spans BRIDGES

Sage-green **Liberty Bridge** (MAP: ❺ P50 **D4**) is one of Budapest's most stunning bridges thanks to its striking colour and ornamental crisscross metalwork. It began life in 1896 as Franz Joseph Bridge, and the Habsburg emperor himself hammered the last silver rivet into the structure – note the miniature guerilla statue of Franz Joseph in a hammock on the northern side. Like all the other bridges across the Danube, Liberty Bridge was blown up during WWII. It was the first to be rebuilt in its original style and was renamed at the same time.

The first bridge to be rebuilt in a new design was the slender and elegant **Elizabeth Bridge** (MAP: ❻ P50 **C2**), in 1964. This version is wider than the original and suspension technology replaced the earlier chains. It's named after the Hungarians' favourite queen, Habsburg empress Elizabeth (1837–98), affectionately known as Sissi. A statue by the foot of the bridge on the Buda side honours her.

Pass by Budapest's Narrowest Building APARTMENT BUILDING

MAP: ❼ P50 **C2**

It will take you only eight steps to walk past **Budapest's narrowest building** on the banks of the Danube under Várkert Rakpart 16. Built in 1897 with a gorgeous neo-Gothic facade, the apartment building is only 6.2m wide – or is it Grimmauld Place from Harry Potter?

Take a Trip Back in Time in Tabán NOTABLE BUILDINGS

Already inhabited in Neolithic times due to its great geological gifts, Tabán started out as a prominent winemaking village that first become part of Buda and later

---

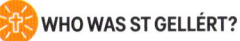 **WHO WAS ST GELLÉRT?**

A hill, a bath, a hotel, a square and a metro station in the neighbourhood are all named after one man: St Gellért. But who was this guy? Gellért was an Italian missionary who ended up in Hungary around 1020. King Stephen convinced him to stay to convert the masses to Christianity. After being named a bishop, he went on to live the life of a hermit. Legend has it that after the king died in 1038, the pagan Magyars hurled the bishop to his death in a spiked barrel. His statue now stands on the spot of his martyrdom, gazing peacefully down onto the city.

Budapest. By the 20th century, it was considered 'Budapest's Montmartre', a bohemian district characterised by winding streets swarming with single-storey buildings glued together, wineries and brothels – a perfect haunt for Budapest's artists and literaries. In the 1930s, Tabán was completely demolished because of its outdated infrastructure and unsanitary conditions, and though several grandiose plans aimed to rebuild it as a modern district, none were ever realised and today Tabán is nothing but a huge green park. A few buildings do still safeguard its jolly, village-like atmosphere, such as the **Semmelweis House** (p58), **Aranyszarvas** restaurant (MAP: ❽ P50 B1), the oldest building in Tabán housing three restaurants under the name **ODA** (p61), and the **Virág Benedek House** (MAP: ❾ P50 B1), a cultural centre with a lovely garden that's home to a century-old tree.

Be Stunned at SkyDeck SKYSCRAPER

MAP: ❿ P50 E8

A politically controversial building in south Buda, the **MOL Campus** *(molcampus.hu)* stands tall on BudaPart Kopaszi-gát as the city's first skyscraper. For an entry fee, you can peer out from the 120m-high **SkyDeck** *(adult/student 2400/1400Ft)* lookout tower for a real bird's eye view of Budapest.

Rock Out at A38 CONCERT VENUE

MAP: ⓫ P50 F7

South from the Gellért Hill district lies one of the city's coolest concert spaces. Moored by the foot of Petőfi Bridge, **A38** *(a38.hu)* is a major live-music venue on a decommissioned 1968 Ukrainian cargo ship.

Picnic by the Bottomless Lake PUBLIC PARK

MAP: ⓬ P50 B7

The **Bottomless Lake** (Feneketlen tó) and its surroundings make for one of Buda's favourite parks. While the name suggests that the lake plunges deep into Earth's crust, it's actually only 4m to 5m deep. It's the perfect place for a quick picnic or more active recreation. Don't miss the statue of the bear, standing strong since 1961, which always has something in its paws – the neighbourhood children ensure that it's never without a gift or two.

Mingle with Locals at Bartók Béla Út STREET

Named after one of Hungary's most famous composers, **Bartók Béla út** (MAP: ⓭ P50 D4) is the trendiest strip in the district, especially between Szent Gellért tér and Móricz Zsigmond körtér, where it's full of offbeat bars, cafes, restaurants and galleries. Look out for **Zsiráf Tranzit** (p61), set up in a former bus depot, or historic **Hadik** (p61) and its adjacent **Szatyor** (MAP: ⓮ P50 D6) ruin bar.

LISTINGS

Best Places for...

€ Budget €€ Midrange €€€ Top End

Eating

Dinner Spots

Búsuló Juhász €€
 B4

Located on Gellért Hill, this restaurant offers amazing views, delicious local food and live piano music. *noon-10pm Tue-Sun*

Felix Kitchen & Bar €€€
 B1

Worth a visit for its imposing building, designed in 1878 as a pump house for the Royal Palace. Serves creative international dishes. *11.30am-midnight*

ODA €€
 A2

Lovely, rustic restaurant in Tabán's oldest building. Brunch, pizzas, schnitzel and bao buns all feature. *8am-10pm Mon-Thu & Sun, to midnight Fri & Sat*

Vegan Love €
 D5

Vegan street food in a hole-in-the-wall restaurant. Try the chilli tofu hotdog. *11am-9pm*

Neapolitan Pizza

Moto Pizza €
 D6

Try traditional Neapolitan pizzas while admiring the shop's green Austin Cooper (a nod to *The Italian Job*). *11.30am-10pm*

Amore di Napoli €
 D6

The blue-and-white interior honours the SSC Napoli football team. *hours vary*

Drinking

Cafes

Kelet Café & Gallery
 D6

Rich coffee, Asian-inspired dishes, Czech beers and a book exchange with thousands of titles. *7.30am-11pm Mon-Fri, 9am-11pm Sat, to 10pm Sun*

Hadik
 D6

A classic Budapest coffee house favoured by artists. Adjacent Szatyor Bár is Buda's take on the ruin-bar theme. *noon-11pm Sun-Wed, to midnight Thu-Sat*

See p50 for map of locations

Bars

Béla
 D5

Great range of wine, local craft beers and meals from breakfast to tapas. *noon-11pm Mon, Tue & Sun, to midnight Wed-Sat*

Palack Borbár
 D5

An impressive selection of wines, mostly from smaller vineyards. Ask the sommelier for advice. *noon-11pm Mon & Tue, to midnight Wed-Sat, to 10pm Sun*

Zsiráf Tranzit
25 A7

This cool, laid-back bar is in a former bus depot. *4-11pm Tue-Fri, noon-11pm Sat & Sun*

Shopping

Local Designs

Prezent
26 C2

Shop specialising in 'sustainable Hungarian design'. Sells fashion, accessories and natural cosmetics. *10am-6pm*

★ WORTH A TRIP

Memento Park

Sneak a peek behind the Iron Curtain at this huge open-air park that guards gigantic statues of Lenin, Marx, Engels and homegrown red-star heroes, along with other types of communist propaganda removed from the streets of Budapest after the fall of the regime in 1989.

Follow the Red-Brick Road

You can visit **Memento Park** on your own or with a private or group guided tour (11.15am Friday to Sunday). The park's antique-style entryway (pictured) displays the communist ideologists Marx and Engels on one side, and Lenin's bronze statue on the other. The ticket office doubles as a quirky gift shop selling all sorts of communist memorabilia, including candles and propaganda posters.

To the right of the ticket office, you can sit inside an old Trabant – a classic East German car that was a dream for many Hungarian families during communism – and eavesdrop on the communist hotline to hear the voices of Joseph Stalin, Mao Zedong and even Che Guevara. To the left is a map that gives you a recommended route for exploring the park.

Ghosts of Communism Past

Once inside, the trophies of Soviet-era sculpting are systematically organised. The centrepiece is a five-point red star made of flower beds, with paths winding in figure-eight patterns. Don't miss the **Statue of the Liberating Soviet Soldier** and the **Hungarian-Soviet Friendship Memorial**.

When Stalin Got the Boot

Opposite the main entrance, you'll find the park's principal attraction: a pair of gigantic boots. They

PLANNING TIPS
Memento Park is open every day of the year. Take M4 to Kelenföld pályaudvar and then bus 101B, 101E or 150 to the Memento Park stop.

Scan this QR code for full opening hours, tours and tickets.

IRENA IRIS SZEWCZYK/SHUTTERSTOCK ©

are a replica of the 8m-high bronze statue of Stalin that was pulled down from its plinth on Dózsa György út in City Park during the 1956 Uprising and sawed apart until only the boots remained. Climb the stairs behind the monument to reach a balcony with a great view of the park entrance. It's the very spot from which communist leaders once waved to crowds below. Inside the plinth, there's a small exhibition of busts, including one of Lenin as a child, as well as temporary displays.

In front, a wooden barrack covers the events of the 1956 Uprising and 1989 regime change, as well as fascinating footage of Hungary's secret police in training – note the handy tips on how to spy on 'enemies of the state'.

ARRIVE IN STYLE
Book a Trabant transfer anytime during opening hours and combine it with a red-themed tour to other communist relics at **Kerepesi Cemetery** (p134) or **Ecseri Piac** (p135).

Explore
Óbuda & the Buda Hills

The narrow streets of Budapest's oldest district, Óbuda, are home to a number of interesting museums that introduce the city's history and art, though the ruins of Aquincum, the capital of the Roman province Pannonia Inferior nearly 2000 years ago, are the main reason people venture to this otherwise quiet neighbourhood. The Buda Hills are the locals' favourite hiking destination with lofty views, a variety of trails and fun forms of transport. Easily accessible from Széll Kálmán tér, the hills are the perfect place to leave the city's buzz behind for some peace, greenery and fresh air. Beneath the hills, exciting caving adventures await.

Getting Around

Óbuda
To reach Óbuda, hop on trams 17, 19 or 41, or the H5 HÉV suburban railway from Batthyány tér or Margit híd and head towards Szentendre. The journey from the city centre will take roughly 30 minutes.

Buda Hills
To head into the Buda Hills, start from Széll Kálmán tér and take bus 21 or 21A to Normafa, which is a great entry point. Once there, you can try various forms of transport, such as the Children's Railway, the Cogwheel Railway or the chairlift.

★

THE BEST

HISTORIC SIGHT Aquincum (p68)

CAVING ADVENTURE Pál-völgy Cave (p72)

HISTORIC BATH Lukács Baths (p73)

QUIRKY MUSEUM Hungarian Museum of Trade and Hospitality (p74)

VANTAGE POINT Elizabeth Lookout Tower (p72)

Children's Railway (p69)
ZGPHOTOGRAPHY/SHUTTERSTOCK ©

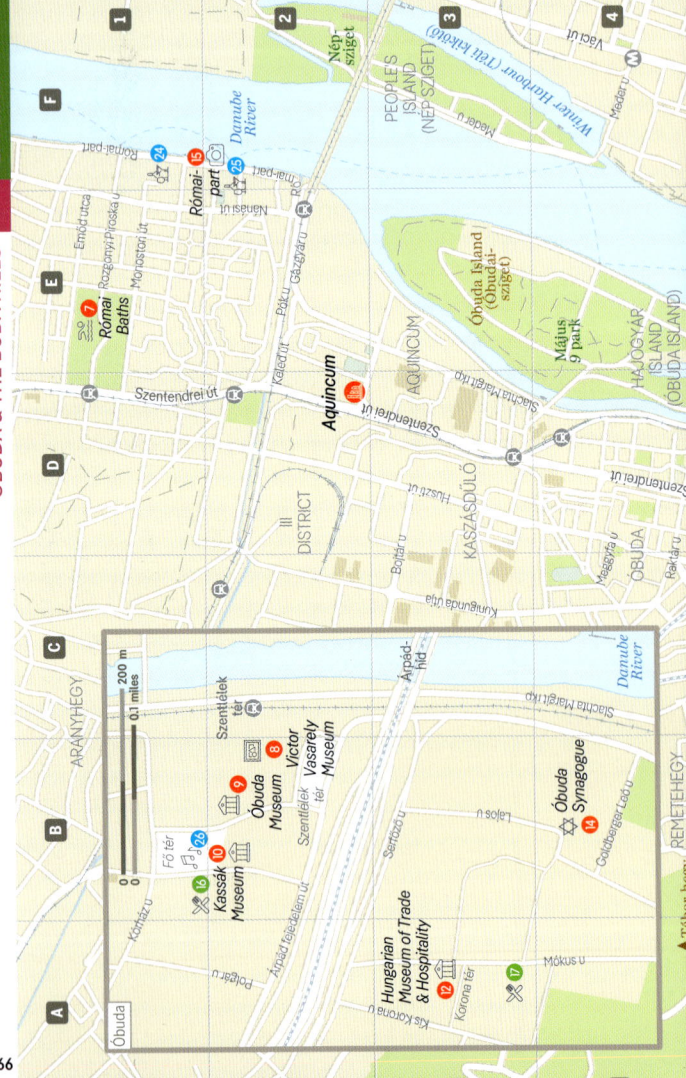

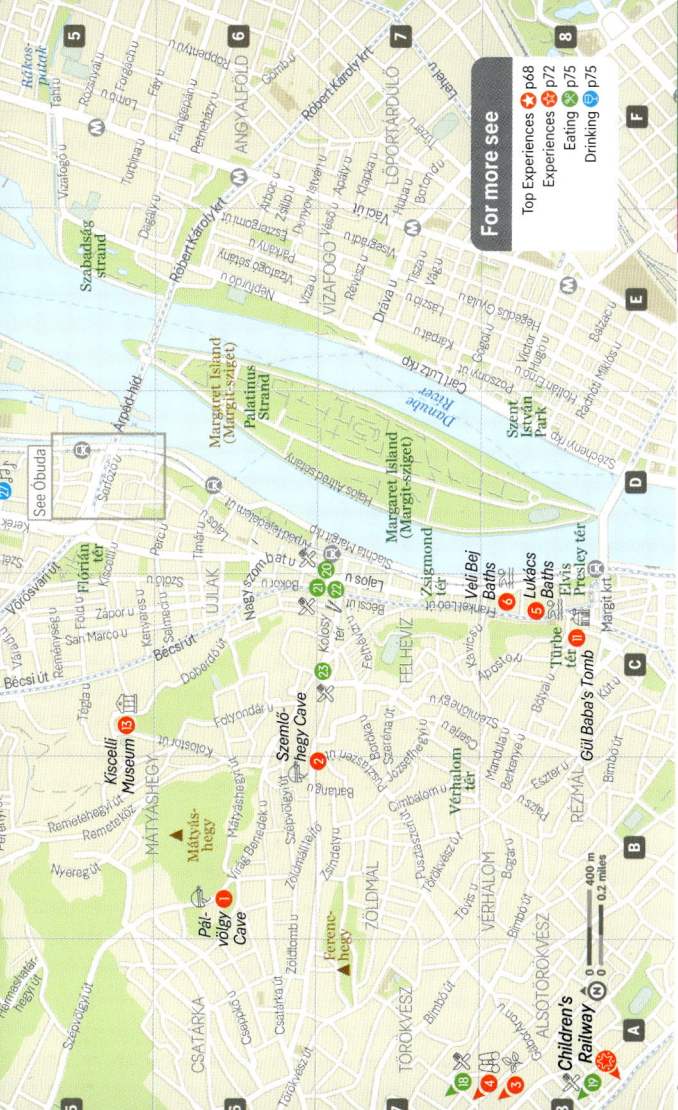

⭐ **TOP EXPERIENCE**

Aquincum

Dating from the 1st century CE, Aquincum is the most complete Roman town in Hungary. It had paved walkways, houses, courtyards, fountains and intricate mosaic floors, and though it's not all immediately apparent as you explore the ruins in the open-air archaeological park, the museum puts it into perspective.

MAP: P66 **D2**

PLANNING TIP
To reach Aquincum, take the H5 suburban train. View the Roman Civilian Amphitheatre first before crossing busy Szentendrei út. Alternatively, hop on bus 34, 106 or 134 to Záhony utca.

Scan this QR code for full opening hours and tickets.

Aquincum Museum

Next to the entrance, the **site museum** contains an impressive collection of household objects such as pottery, weaponry, grooming implements and a map of the Roman empire. Visitors can even battle (virtually) with a gladiator. Look for the replica of a 3rd-century portable organ called a hydraulis.

Remarkable Ruins

Opposite the museum stands the pretty **Painter's House**, a re-created and furnished Roman dwelling from the 3rd century adorned with wall paintings. Behind the Painter's House is the **Mithraeum**, a temple dedicated to the god Mithras, the chief deity of a mysterious Roman religion. North of the museum, take a stroll along the main thoroughfare to see the spacious public baths, the market and the forum.

Hercules Villa

Across Szentendrei út at Meggyfa utca 21 lies the **Hercules Villa**, unearthed in 1958. One of Hungary's best-preserved ruins from the era, it was the mansion of an unknown member of Aquincum's aristocracy. This lavish complex had luxuries such as running water, heated floors, a sewer system and varied chambers for private use, as well as mosaics depicting many intricately crafted characters, including boxers and a tipsy Hercules.

★ **TOP EXPERIENCE**

Children's Railway

Operated almost entirely by kids, the Children's Railway chugs past some of the Buda Hills' most superb hiking spots. Taking a ride is a time-transcending and unique journey, and the staff are among the nicest you'll meet in Hungary.

MAP: P66 **A8**

Sweet Staff

Children aged 10 to 14, dressed in smart blue, white and red uniforms, hold all the positions on the railway, from conductors to signallers, while a little adult supervision keeps things on track (the engineers, thankfully, are grown-ups).

World's Longest

Running from Hűvösvölgy to Széchenyi Hill, taking in forested **Normafa** (p72) on the way, this is the world's longest narrow-gauge children's railway line, earning it an inclusion in Guinness World Records.

Communist Memento

The Children's Railway is a living memento of the communist era. Opened in 1948, it was originally operated by Soviet pioneer scouts. The goal was to give children the chance to learn about teamwork and responsibility. Today, a job on the railway is a prestigious position – only top students are considered, and those selected have to participate in training and exams. Get your tickets ready for Hungary's cutest conductors!

If you'd like to learn more about the railway, check out a short and sweet interactive exhibit and museum shop at Hűvösvölgy Station, showcasing archival photos, documents, relics and games.

PLANNING TIP
Tickets for the Children's Railway can only be purchased at stations or from conductors on the train. Payment is cash only in Hungarian forints.

Scan this QR code for full opening hours and tickets.

Tour the Buda Hills

There are many reasons to head for Budapest's hills: great hiking, unbelievable views and a couple of trip-worthy sights. Locals come for barbecues, long walks and relaxation. With fun forms of transport on offer, getting to and from the Buda Hills is more than half the fun, so hopping aboard some of the way is a must.

START	END	LENGTH
Széll Kálmán tér	Zugligeti út	3km walking; two hours

1 A Nostalgic Ride

Start from Széll Kálmán tér station on the M2 and walk along Szilágyi Erzsébet fasor for about 10 minutes to the lower terminus of the **Cogwheel Railway** (tram 60) opposite the cylindrical Hotel Budapest, an iconic example of Brutalist architecture. The railway's historic red-and-white carriages are a nostalgic sight and will take you the 4km to Széchenyi Hill in style.

2 Children in Charge

Cross the grassy field to Hegyhát út, where you can change to the **Children's Railway** (p69). This lovely little train chugs past excellent excursion spots for about 45 minutes (11km), terminating at Hűvösvölgy. Buy your ticket on board from the young conductors. Walking trails fan out from any of the railway's nine stations.

3 Views, Hikes & Snacks

Get off at the third stop, Virágvölgy, to find yourself near Anna Meadow in the heart of **Normafa** (p72), a year-round destination and forested hill providing ample opportunity for peace and quiet while busy Budapest stretches out below. There are plenty of food stalls around – try a Hungarian *lángos* (disc-shaped deep-fried dough traditionally topped with sour cream and shredded cheese) or *rétes* (flaky sweet pastry).

4 Budapest's Highest Point

From Normafa, you'll see the wonderful wedding-cake-shaped **Elizabeth Lookout Tower** (p72) topping János Hill, the highest point (527m) in Budapest. Follow the leafy, shaded trail heading towards it, then climb the 100-step spiral staircase for remarkable views of Budapest, the surrounding countryside and, on a clear day, even the Tatra Mountains in Slovakia.

5 Stay Aboard

If you prefer to stay on the train, there are five more stops after Normafa, including János Hill, Vadaspark in the middle of the Budakeszi Wildlife Park and Hűvösvölgy, which has a brief but fun interactive exhibit about the Children's Railway's past and present and a museum shop.

6 A Breezy Ride

About 700m south of the Elizabeth Lookout Tower is the upper station of the chairlift, which will take you the 1040m down to Zugligeti út in 15 minutes while providing wonderful panoramas of the Buda surroundings and a sneak peek into some locals' gardens on the way. From Zugligeti út, bus 291 heads back to the city, terminating at Nyugati railway station.

EXPERIENCES

Explore Budapest's Caves
CAVES

Rich in dripstone and stalagmite formations, **Pál-völgy Cave** (MAP: ① P66 B6; *dunaipoly.hu; adult/student 3500/2600Ft*) is Hungary's longest cave system, with subterranean passages extending over 32km. Hourly 60-minute tours depart between 10.15am and 4.15pm every day (except Monday) – an English audio guide is available. If you want the full spelunking experience, leave the well-trodden paths behind for an exciting three-hour caving tour *(caving.hu; 19,900Ft)* with lots of crawling and scrambling in protective coveralls and headgear at the Mátyás Hill Cave.

Those looking for an easier – and partially wheelchair accessible – tour can explore nearby **Szemlő-hegy Cave** (MAP: ② P66 B7; *dunaipoly.hu; adult/student 3400/2600Ft*), which, instead of stalactites, provides lots of sparkle. The cave's walls are lined with crystals and minerals, which shimmer beautifully. Hourly 40-minute tours depart between 10am and 4pm daily (except Tuesday).

Hike around Normafa
PUBLIC PARK

MAP: ③ P66 A8

Normafa is a forested hill in the Buda Hills, within the city limits and easily accessible on public transport. It offers huge green spaces, hiking trails, a playground, food stalls, gorgeous views, picnic spots and designated barbecue pits, providing a perfect place to unwind while overlooking the capital. It offers something for every season: spring sees cherry blossoms; summer offers hikes and family picnics; autumn has vibrant foliage; and winter allows sledging on the Anna Meadow.

Climb to Budapest's Highest Point
LOOKOUT TOWER

MAP: ④ P66 A8

The **Elizabeth Lookout Tower** is a short but steep walk from Normafa. Topping 527m-high János Hill, the neo-Roman tower is Budapest's highest point. Thanks to a dazzling design by Frigyes Schulek, who also conceived Fisherman's Bastion, it resembles a three-tier wedding cake and is named after Hungary's beloved Queen Sissi. To get to the top,

---

 FREE YOUR MIND AT SZIGET FESTIVAL

Every August, Óbuda Island becomes the 'Island of Freedom', hosting Hungary's biggest annual bash. At **Sziget Festival** *(szigetfestival.com),* concerts and musical performances by the hottest headliners and up-and-coming acts go from early afternoon through to dawn. The five-day festival also features art performances, film screenings, a makeshift beach, a funfair, photo booths and bungee jumping.

you must climb up a 100-step spiral staircase, but the 360-degree panorama will make up for the effort.

Splash Around at Historic Baths   BATHS AND LIDOS

In a lovely 19th-century building, medicinal **Lukács Baths** (MAP: ❺ P66 C8; *lukacsfurdo.hu; adult/student 5200/4500Ft*) is one of the city's longest-standing spas. Its thermal waters are said to be the highest quality of all Budapest's baths.

Less grand than the city's other baths, **Veli Bej Baths** (MAP: ❻ P66 C8; *irgalmasrend.hu; admission 4500-5500Ft*) are perfect for those wanting to avoid crowds. The interior is a mixture of old and new: the 16th-century Turkish bath's original walls and water pipes are still on display, though much of the interior has been renovated with modern touches. No under-14s.

For family fun, go for summer-only **Római Baths** (MAP: ❼ P66 E1; *romaistrand.hu; adult/student 4000/3400Ft*), equipped with winding water slides, a kids' pool and playground. The thermal spring that fills this lido was a known water source in Roman times, when the grounds were regarded as a holy site – archaeologists found the ruins of a sanctuary here.

Find Three Museums at the Zichy Mansion   MUSEUMS

The beautiful 18th-century Baroque Zichy Mansion is home to three interesting museums. The **Victor Vasarely Museum** (MAP: ❽ P66 B2; *vasarely.hu; adult/student 2400/1200Ft*) displays some 150 works by the 'grandfather of op-art', who was born as Győző Vásárhelyi in 1906 in Pécs. His visually arresting pieces trick the mind with illusions of depth and motion.

A separate entrance leads to the **Óbuda Museum** (MAP: ❾ P66 B2; *obudaimuzeum.hu; adult/student 1400/700Ft*), where you can learn about the district's intriguing history, from medieval times to the present day. The interactive exhibits test four of your senses – sight, hearing, smell and touch – and encourage you to get creative.

The third site within the villa's walls is the **Kassák Museum** (MAP: ❿ P66 B2; *kassakmuzeum.hu; adult/student 1200/600Ft*), which presents the intellectual legacy of Lajos Kassák, a celebrated writer, poet and editor of the 1920s Hungarian avant-garde.

Forget You're in Budapest at Gül Baba's Tomb   TOMB AND GARDENS

MAP: ⓫ P66 C8

As you walk up the cobbled Gül Baba utca, you won't just feel like you're in another country – you might even wonder if you've travelled back in time. At the top of the street is the octagonal **Gül Baba's Tomb**, a popular pilgrimage site for Muslims, especially from Turkey. Gül Baba was a 16th-century dervish poet who took part in the capture of Buda in 1541 and is known in Hungary as the 'Father of Roses'. Be sure to remove your shoes before entering. The surrounding rose and lavender gardens are the perfect spot to escape the buzz of Budapest and admire the panorama. The Cultural Centre and Exhibition Hall takes a closer look at Ottoman culture and its legacy in Budapest.

Check out the Hungarian Museum of Trade & Hospitality   MUSEUM
MAP: 12 P66 A3

Despite the uninspired name, the **Museum of Trade & Hospitality** (*mkvm.hu; adult/student 3000/2000Ft*) is a fun little place. It traces Hungary's catering and hospitality through the ages, displaying restaurant items, tableware, advertising posters, shop signs, furniture and photographs. Peek into the early 20th century through a variety of interiors: a hotel room, cafe, restaurant, confectioner and a middle-class family home. You can also play interactive games, test your wine knowledge as a sommelier and learn the stories of the most famous Hungarian dishes. You can even take some original recipes home.

Find Treasures at the Kiscelli Museum   MUSEUM
MAP: 13 P66 C5

The **Kiscelli Museum** (*kiscellimuzeum.hu; adult/student 3000/1500Ft*), housed in an 18th-century, daffodil-yellow Baroque monastery and church, manages a vast collection of objects related to the urban history of Budapest. Enter a complete 19th-century pharmacy and admire an impressive display of signboards advertising shops and other trades, silver artefacts and rooms equipped with Empire, Biedermeier and Art Nouveau furniture. The stark church used for temporary multimedia and art exhibits is visually arresting.

Mavel at the Óbuda Synagogue   SYNAGOGUE
MAP: 14 P66 B4

Built in 1821, at a time when the Jewish community in Óbuda was one of the largest in the country, the **Óbuda Synagogue** (*obudaizsinagoga.hu*) is Budapest's oldest synagogue. For many years, the building housed Hungarian TV sound studios because the much-reduced post-WWII Jewish population couldn't afford the upkeep, but it is once again functioning as a *súl* (Jewish prayer house) with workshops and services. The synagogue is a superb example of the classical architectural style in Hungary. Call ahead for a tour.

Roam around Római-part   RIVERSIDE
MAP: 15 P66 F1

Riverside **Római-part** (Római Shore) is at the northern tip of Buda. It's a popular weekend destination for kayaking, canoeing and stand-up paddle boarding – all available to rent – or just sitting by the river in a colourful deck chair with some hake (Hungary's version of fish and chips) or *lángos*. Római-part is 20 minutes away from the city centre and easily accessible by bike or public transport.

LISTINGS

Best Places for...

🅖 Budget 🅖🅖 Midrange 🅖🅖🅖 Top End

Eating

Hungarian

Csalánosi Csárda 🅖🅖
16 B1

Old-fashioned restaurant with homestyle cooking, traditional recipes, authentic flavours and hearty portions. *9am-midnight*

Kéhli Vendéglő 🅖🅖
17 A3

Self-consciously rustic, Kéhli is known for its 19th-century atmosphere and some of the best traditional Hungarian food in town. *noon-10pm Mon-Fri & Sun, to 10.30pm Sat*

Náncsi Néni 🅖🅖
18 A7

Aunty Náncsi's is much beloved by both locals and expats. The Hűvösvölgy restaurant specialises in game in autumn and winter, plus goose-liver dishes. *noon-10pm*

Normafa Síház 🅖🅖🅖
19 A8

A lovely restaurant at forested Normafa, offering local and international dishes, delicious drinks and all kinds of thematic summer events summer. *hours vary*

International Fare

Semmi Extra 🅖🅖
20 D7

A spacious, fuss-free eatery serving burgers, wraps, pastas and special lunch deals. *hours vary*

Hummus Bar 🅖
21 C7

Fresh Middle Eastern delights such as shakshuka and falafel bring in the crowds on Kolosy tér. *11am-10pm Mon-Fri, noon-10pm Sat & Sun*

Okuyama no Sushi 🅖🅖
22 C7

Tiny Japanese restaurant tucked away in the basement of the Kolosy Üzletház (department store). Arguably the best sushi in town. *11am-10pm*

Sweets

Daubner Cukrászda 🅖🅖🅖
23 C7

Locals come to this cafe dating to 1901 for its macarons, traditional Hungarian cakes and *pogácsa* (savoury scones). *noon-7pm Wed, 9am-7pm Thu-Sun*

See p66 for map of locations

Drinking

Summertime Picks

Fellini Római
24 F1

Lounge about in striped riverfront deck chairs while your feet touch the Danube at Római-part. *hours vary*

Két Rombusz
25 F2

Sit inside (or atop) two old buses or enjoy a hammock in the shade, with the river in arm's reach. *hours vary*

Kert
26 B1

Open-air Kobuci is an atmospheric live-music venue, with scores of cool Hungarian bands on stage. *hours vary*

Mad Garden Óbuda
27 D5

Street food and craft beer from the renowned Mad Scientist brewery in a lovely garden. *hours vary*

See p84 for eating, drinking and shopping listings

Explore Belváros

The 'Inner Town' is the centre of Pest's universe, especially for high-end tourism and shopping. This is where you'll find Váci utca, with its luxury shops, restaurants and bars, and Vörösmarty tér, home to the city's most celebrated *cukrászda* (cake shop). The area's centre is busy Deák Ferenc tér, the main square where three of the city's four metro lines converge. Belváros has two sides to its personality. The area north of busy Ferenciek tere is full of flashy boutiques and well-frequented bars and restaurants. The neighbourhood to the south is more student-driven, quieter and local, with much of it reserved for pedestrians. Still, there's an increasing number of trendy cafes and restaurants here too, along with the usual souvenir shops and independent stores.

Getting Around

 Metro
At the heart of Belváros, Deák Ferenc tér is conveniently served by three metro lines (M1/2/3).

 Tram
Tram 2 (or 2B or 23) heads along the district's western edge by the Danube. Trams 47 and 49 follow the eastern perimeter of the Inner Town from Deák Ferenc tér then cross Liberty Bridge to points in south Buda.

 Bus
Useful buses from Ferenciek tere include the 7 (or 7E) to Buda and the 15 to northern Pest.

THE BEST

ARCHITECTURE Párisi Udvar (p81)

VIEWPOINT South Tower of Inner Town Parish Church (p83)

CONCERT VENUE Pesti Vigadó (p82)

BAR FOR LATE NIGHTS Why Not Cafe (p85)

PARK TO CHILL IN Károly Garden (p83)

Párisi Udvar (p81)
MITZO/SHUTTERSTOCK ©

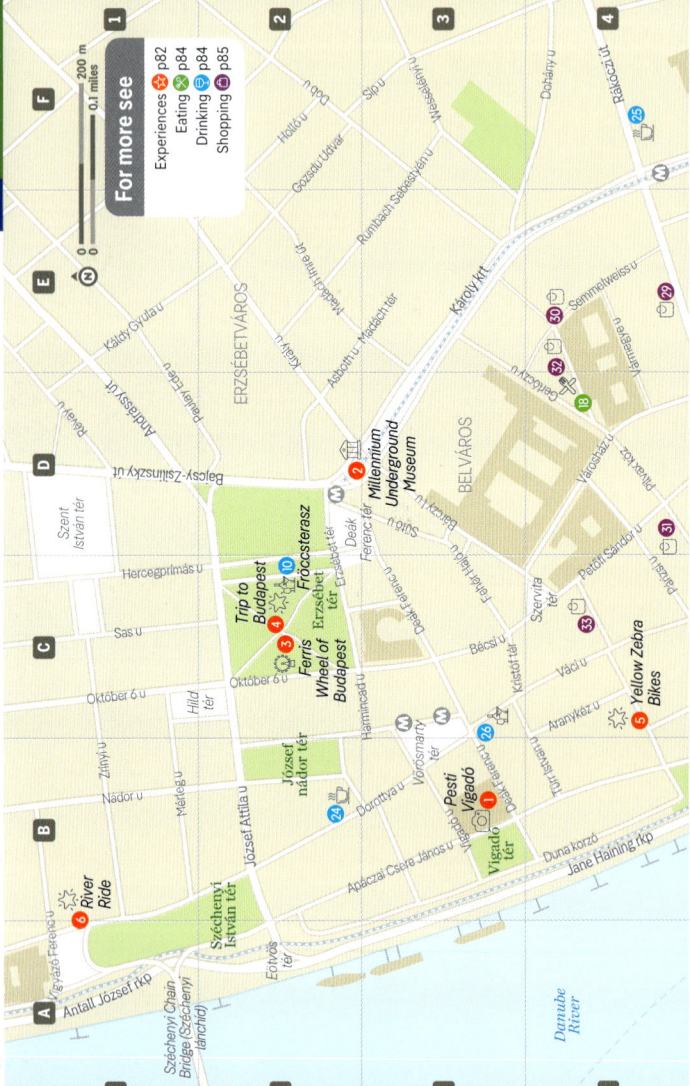

BELVÁROS — EXPLORE

Map locations:

- Károly Garden (7)
- Csendes Létterem (22)
- Inner Town Parish Church (9)

Streets and landmarks:
- Múzeum krt
- Baross u
- Üllői út
- Ráday u
- Kálvin tér
- Vámház krt
- Török Pál u
- Erkel u
- Lónyay u
- Göncz P u
- Imre u
- Pipa u
- Magyar u
- Szentkirályi u
- Királyi Pál u
- Kecskeméti u
- Reáltanoda u
- Henszlmann Imre u
- Egyetem tér
- Szerb u
- Ferenczy István u
- Szép u
- Fehér György u
- Szerb u
- Corvinus University of Budapest
- Fővám tér
- Kossuth Lajos u
- Károlyi Mihály u
- Cukor u
- Szivárvány u
- Veres Pálné u
- Nyáry Pál u
- Havas u
- Molnár u
- Ferenciek tere
- Szabad sajtó út
- Váci u
- Duna u
- Vám u
- Vámház krt
- Molnár u
- Belgrád rkp
- Liberty Bridge (Szabadság híd)
- Galamb u
- Piarista köz
- Piarista u
- Március 15 tér
- Petőfi tér
- Pesti alsó rkp
- Elizabeth Bridge (Erzsébet híd)
- Friedrich Born rkp
- Szent Gellért rkp
- Döbrentei tér
- Jubilee Park
- Bartók Béla út
- GELLÉRT HILL (GELLÉRT-HEGY)
- Citadel
- JÓZSEFVÁROS

WALKING TOUR

Walk Váci Utca & Vörösmarty Tér

The capital's premier shopping street, Váci utca, is a pedestrian strip crammed largely with chain stores, touristy restaurants and a smattering of shops and notable buildings worth seeking out. It was the total length of the city of Pest in the Middle Ages. Delightful Vörösmarty tér is at its northern end.

START	END	LENGTH
Ferenciek tere	Duna korzó	1.3km; one to two hours

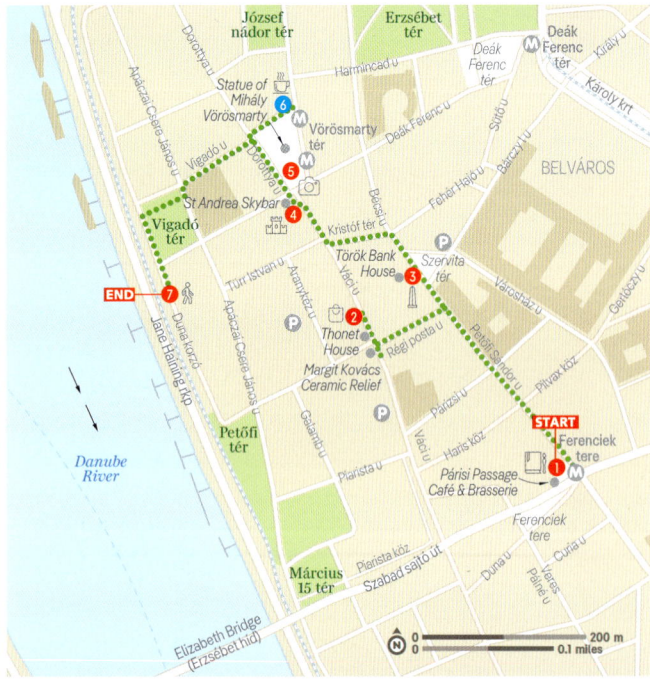

1 Stunning Architecture

Start at Párisi Udvar. Built in 1909, this is a stunning, ornate example of eclectic architecture, with Moorish, Gothic and Art Nouveau elements. It was for decades a delightful but down-at-heel shopping arcade but has received a total top-to-bottom renovation and now houses several eateries and a 110-room hotel. Walk through the ground-level public area and have a drink at the **Párisi Passage Café & Brasserie** (p84). Váci utca is immediately west.

2 Floral Delights

Head up Petőfi Sándor utca and turn left onto Régi posta utca. At No 15, there's a ceramic relief of an old postal coach by the celebrated Szentendre artist Margit Kovács. Continue along Váci utca to **Philanthia**, a flower shop with a rare Art Nouveau interior from 1906. Next door, **Thonet House** is a masterpiece built by Ödön Lechner in 1890.

3 Mother Hungary Mosaic

Around the corner to the east, facing Szervita tér, is **Török Bank House**, built in 1906, with a glass-covered facade. In the upper gable, there's a Secessionist mosaic by Miksa Róth called *Patrona Hungariae*, which depicts the 'patroness' Hungary and her most celebrated Magyar sons.

4 At the Bank

Back on Váci utca is the sumptuous **Bank Palace**, built in 1915 and once the home of the Budapest Stock Exchange. It has since been converted into a shopping gallery called Váci1, with the Hard Rock Cafe as anchor tenant and the wonderful **St Andrea Skybar** (p85) on its roof.

5 The Prettiest Square

Váci utca opens into **Vörösmarty tér**, a large square of smart shops, galleries, cafes and artists who will draw your portrait or caricature. In the centre is a statue of Mihály Vörösmarty, the 19th-century poet after whom the square is named. Made of a brittle Italian marble, the sculpture is protected in winter by a bizarre plastic 'iceberg' on which kids love sliding.

6 Designer Cake

At the northern end of the square is **Gerbeaud**, Budapest's most famous patisserie. Grab a seat on the terrace and order the Dobos torta, a seven-layer chocolate-buttercream sponge topped with caramelised sugar, invented by Hungarian confectioner József C Dobos in 1884.

7 The Long Walk

A pleasant way to end the walk is to stroll along the **Duna korzó**, the riverside 'Danube Promenade' between Chain and Elizabeth bridges.

EXPERIENCES

Listen to Music in Glamorous Surrounds
CONCERT HALL

MAP: ① P78 B3

The **Pesti Vigadó** *(vigado.hu; adult/concession combined ticket 2500/1250Ft, exhibitions only 1000/500Ft)*, a Romantic-style performing arts venue built in 1865 but badly damaged during WWII, has been fully restored to its former grandeur and is a fantastic place to catch a classical-music performance. The massive concert hall is on the 2nd floor, the theatre is on the 4th floor, and floors 5 and 6 are used for temporary exhibitions. There's also a fantastic terrace with a small cafe affording expansive Danube views.

Ride the Millennial Rail
TRANSPORT MUSEUM

MAP: ② P78 D2

In the pedestrian underpass below Deák Ferenc tér, with its entrance within the main metro ticket office, the small but fascinating **Millennium Underground Museum** *(bkv.hu/en/millennium_underground_museum; adult/concession 900/450Ft)* traces the development of the city's metro lines. Much emphasis is on the little yellow metro (M1), continental Europe's first underground railway, which opened for the millenary celebrations in 1896, marking 1000 years of Hungarian settlement in the Carpathian Basin. The museum is housed in a stretch of tunnel and original station.

Take a Short but Sweet Twirl
FERRIS WHEEL

MAP: ③ P78 C2

Dominating Erzsébet tér, the 65m-high **Ferris Wheel of Budapest** *(oriaskerek.com; adult/concession from 4300/2300Ft)* is less than half the height of the London Eye, and the ride is over in just three revolutions in six to eight minutes, but it does offer wonderful views of

BEST GUIDED TOURS OF BUDAPEST
Trip to Budapest (MAP: ④ P78 C2; *triptobudapest.hu*) offers 'free' two-hour walking tours of Budapest's top sights in English; guides work for tips only. **Yellow Zebra Bikes** (MAP: ⑤ P78 C4; *yellowzebrabikes.com; from 18,300Ft*) has four-hour guided cycle tours taking in Heroes' Square, City Park, central Pest and Buda via Margaret Bridge. **Tuk Tuk Taxi** *(tuktuktaxi.hu; from 24,400Ft)* has popular guided tours that whisk two or three people around in Bangkok-style three-wheelers. More exhilarating than conventional boat trips on the Danube is high-speed **RedJet** (p58; *redjet.hu; from 5,300Ft*) and the quirky **River Ride** (MAP: ⑥ P78 B1; *riverride.com; adult/student 13,800Ft/11,800Ft*), a bright yellow amphibious bus that takes you on a 1½-hour tour of the city by road and river.

Pest and across the Danube to Buda. It's particularly impressive at night.

Chill in a Quiet Green Space
FLOWER GARDEN

A pleasant place in which to take a breather, flower-filled **Károly Garden** (MAP: 7 P78 E5) was built for the nearby (and stunning) Károly Palace, which houses a literature museum. It's frequented by locals, many with children – it has a lovely playground. The garden is a riot of colourful flowerbeds in summer, and there are plenty of shady benches. **Csendes Társ** (p84), the summer cafe of the **Csendes Létterem** (MAP: 8 P78 F5) ruin bar, is an atmospheric spot for a sundowner or snack, with tables around the park's entrance gate.

Join the Steeple Chase
CHURCH TOWER

MAP: 9 P78 C5

The often-overlooked **Inner Town Parish Church** (belvarosiplebania.hu; adult/concession 3000/2000Ft), sitting uncomfortably close to the Elizabeth Bridge flyover, is worth a visit for no other reason than to ascend the 55m-high South Tower. It was built on the site of a 12th-century Romanesque church, itself situated within a Roman fortress. Gain access to the tower at the end of the south aisle to the right of the main entrance; there's a small lift or you can climb the 98 steps. At the top, cross through a dense network of beams to the North Tower, from where the bells ring.

FAVOURITE BUDAPEST NOVELS
As chosen by Tony Dabbous Láng, founder of **Bestsellers** (bestsellers.hu), the city's finest independent bookshop.

District VIII (Adam LeBor; 2019) This crime novel has a Roma detective investigating from the upscale neighbourhoods of the Buda Hills to gritty District VIII.

The Paul Street Boys (Ferenc Molnár; 1906) Turn-of-the-century novel about a group of boys growing up in the tough Józsefváros district.

Journey by Moonlight (Antal Szerb; 1937) Masterpiece about a young Budapester as he attempts to make sense of his past.

The Door (Magda Szabó; 1987) The narrator of the novel is Magda, a writer. The story focuses on her decades-long relationship with her housekeeper, Emerence.

Something Cooling Down the Hatch
SUMMER DRINKS

MAP: 10 P78 C2

In the summertime, spritzers (*fröccs*) of white wine or rosé mixed with sparkling water are consumed in vast quantities – knowing the hierarchy and the art of mixing a spritzer to taste, from *kisfröccs* (small spritzer) and *nagyfröccs* (big spritzer) to *hosszúlépés* (long step) and *házmester* (janitor), will win you kudos as an honorary local. Try them in the **Fröccsterasz** (froccsterasz.hu) complex in Erzsébet tér.

LISTINGS

Best Places for...

❶ Budget ❷❷ Midrange ❸❸❸ Top End

Eating

Hungarian

Szeged Halászcsárda ❷❷
11 C7

Serves classic freshwater-fish soup as well as carp, catfish and pikeperch prepared in the spicy Szeged style. A must-try. *11am-9pm Tue-Thu, to 10pm Fri & Sat, to 5pm Sun*

Monk's Bistrot ❷❷
12 C5

Modern reimagining of Hungarian dishes served in industrial surrounds by hip staff. *noon-11pm*

Ruben Restaurant ❷❷
13 F5

This spacious and stylish restaurant is the place for classic national cuisine such as Hortobágy *palacsinta* and roast duck leg. *noon-4pm & 6-10pm*

Mediterranean & Middle Eastern

Taverna Dionysos ❷❷
14 D7

Blue-and-white decor and Greek favourites, from tzatziki and souvlaki to fresh grilled fish. *noon-midnight*

Trattoria La Coppola ❸❸❸
15 E6

Sicilian-owned, this welcoming trattoria is some locals' favourite Italian restaurant for its pasta, pizza and signature *pignata*, a rich seafood stew. *noon-midnight*

Baalbek ❸❸❸
16 C6

Stylish Lebanese by the river, serving favourites such as *kibbeh labanieh* (meat in yoghurt sauce) and lamb kebabs. *noon-midnight Mon-Wed, from 8am Thu-Sun*

Brunch

Deszka ❷❷
17 E7

The always-welcoming 'Board' serves eggs and much more with a twist (touch of Turkish, hint of Japanese) in convivial surrounds. *8.30am-4pm*

Gerlóczy Café ❸❸❸
18 D4

The expanded terrace of this wonderful retro-style cafe sits under a shady linden and looks onto one of Pest's most attractive little squares. *7.30am-11pm*

See p78 for map of locations

Solid ❸❸❸
19 E6

Formerly a chi-chi wine bar atop the Hotel Rum, this is now a fabulous brunch restaurant with the best views in town. *7am-noon Mon-Wed, to 2pm Thu-Sun*

Drinking

Cafes

Párisi Passage Café & Brasserie
20 D5

It's hard to imagine a more sumptuous and magical venue than this cafe in the renovated Párisi Udvar with its glistening tiles and mosaics. *8am-6.30pm*

Centrál Kávéház
21 D5

This grande dame of a traditional cafe dates back to 1887. It's airy and a great spot for people-watching. *9am-10pm Sun-Tue, to midnight Wed-Sat*

Csendes Társ
22 F5

In fine weather, the 'Silent Partner' sets up a terrace around the gates of peaceful Károly Garden and attracts a carefree crowd. *11am-midnight Mon-Fri, from 10am Sat & Sun*

Speciality Coffee

Fekete
 F5

Espresso, macchiato, ristretto, nitro cold brew and a decent menu (till 3pm) facing a large open-air inner courtyard. *8am-7pm*

Edison & Jupiter
B2

This 'coffee lounge and gastrolab' a stone's throw from Vörösmarty tér takes its java seriously. *9am-6pm Sun-Thu, to 8pm Fri & Sat*

Arch & Beans
 F4

The roasting machines work overtime at this beautiful coffee house in a monumental fin-de-siècle arched hall. *8am-6pm Mon-Fri, 9am-6pm Sat, 9am-3pm Sun*

Bars with Views

St Andrea Skybar
 C3

This spacious bar atop the Váciˈl centre (the erstwhile Bank Palace) is just the ticket for dizzying cocktails. *3pm-midnight Mon-Sat, to 10pm Sun*

Why Not Cafe
 D8

Perennial gay/mixed favourite, celebrated for its events and fabulous views of Buda Castle and the river. *11am-5am Mon-Fri, from 10am Sat & Sun*

Port de Budapest
 C6

This attractive eatery (burgers, salads) practically in the Danube is the place to come for affordable riverine cocktails. *noon-midnight*

Shopping

Fashion & Jewellery

Paloma Artspace
 E4

Combining fashion and art, Paloma showcases the work of up-and-coming Hungarian designers and stages contemporary-art exhibitions. *11am-7pm Mon-Fri, to 3pm Sat*

Rododendron
 E4

This delightful shop presents the work of local designers, with everything from jewellery and handbags to unique prints. *11am-7pm Mon-Fri, 10am-6pm Sat & Sun*

Vass Shoes
 D4

Traditional shoemaker stocking high-quality, ready-to-wear shoes. Also cobbles to order. *10am-6pm Mon-Fri, to 4pm Sat*

Folk Art

Holló Műhely
 E4

Our favourite place for Hungarian folk art, though the painted eggs and boxes are heavily influenced by Saxon folk art in Romania. *2-6pm Tue & Thu, 10am-1pm Wed*

Folkart Kézművésház
 C4

Everything Magyar – all of it made here – is available, from embroidered tablecloths to painted eggs and rustic-chic pottery. *10am-6pm Mon-Fri, to 3pm Sat*

Chocolate

Rózsavölgyi Csokoládé
 D5

Boutique in the Párisi Udvar selling award-winning bean-to-bar chocolates handmade locally in unusual flavours. *10.30am-1pm & 1.30-6.30pm Mon-Fri, noon-6pm Sat*

Cadeau
D5

Delectable filled bonbons handmade by a celebrated patisserie in Gyula, in Hungary's southeast. *10am-6pm Mon-Fri*

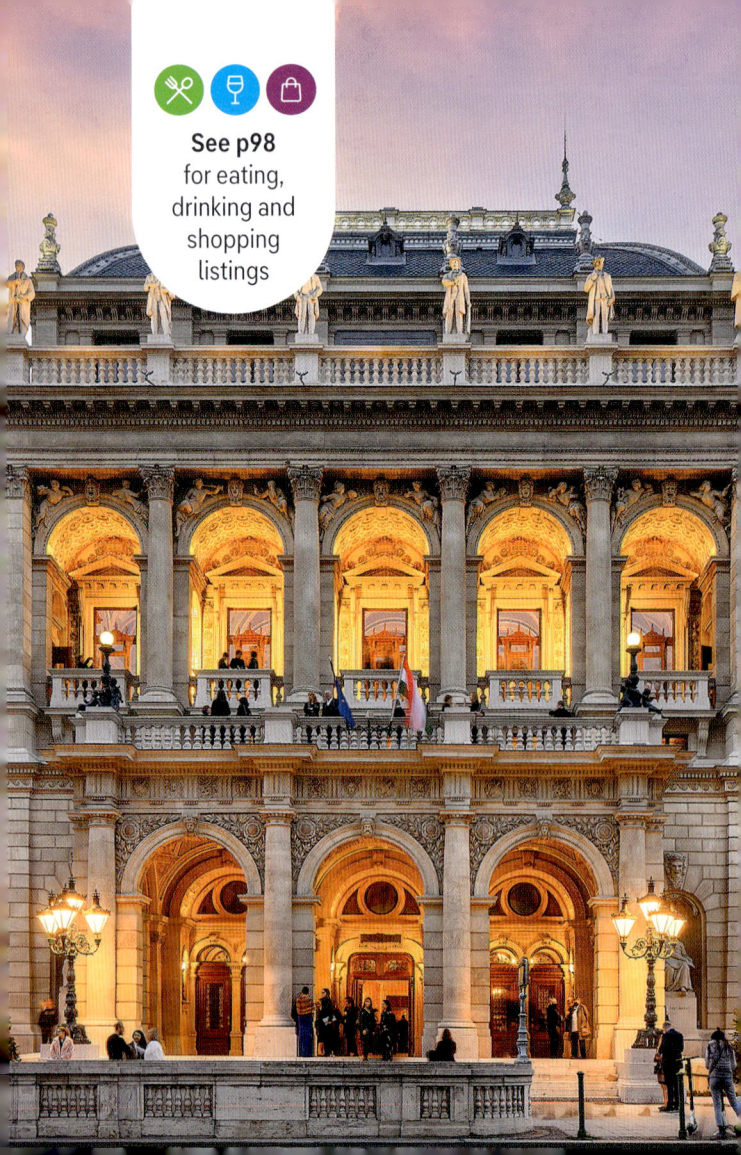

See p98 for eating, drinking and shopping listings

Explore
Parliament & Around

North of Belváros is Lipótváros (Leopold Town), with the landmark Parliament facing the Danube to the northwest and the equally iconic Basilica of St Stephen to the southeast. This is prime sightseeing territory, where you'll also discover great galleries and exhibitions, some lovely squares and Art Nouveau/Secessionist buildings. It's an easy neighbourhood to explore on foot and has excellent high-end restaurants, welcoming cafes and good bars.

East of Lipótváros lies Terézváros (Theresa Town), named in honour of Habsburg empress Maria Theresa. This is a district that gets very busy after dark: here you'll find Nagymező utca – 'Budapest's Broadway', lined with theatres and music halls – as well as the city's largest and most popular gay club.

Getting Around

 Metro
The M2 serves Kossuth Lajos tér (good for the Parliament), while the M3 stops at Arany János just north of the basilica. The M1, M2 and M3 converge at Deák Ference tér, which is a short walk south of the basilica.

 Tram
Trams 2, 2B and 23 run along the Danube at the western edge of this neighbourhood, while trams 4 and 6 serve its northern parts.

 Bus
To reach areas further north in Pest, hop on bus 15 in Kossuth Lajor tér.

THE BEST

ARCHITECTURE Hungarian State Opera House (p97)

PARTYING Alterego (p99)

COMMUNIST REMINDERS Budapest Retro Museum (p97)

ANTIQUE SHOPPING Falk Miksa utca (p96)

SQUARE Szabadság tér (p95)

Hungarian State Opera House (p97)
MITZO/SHUTTERSTOCK ©

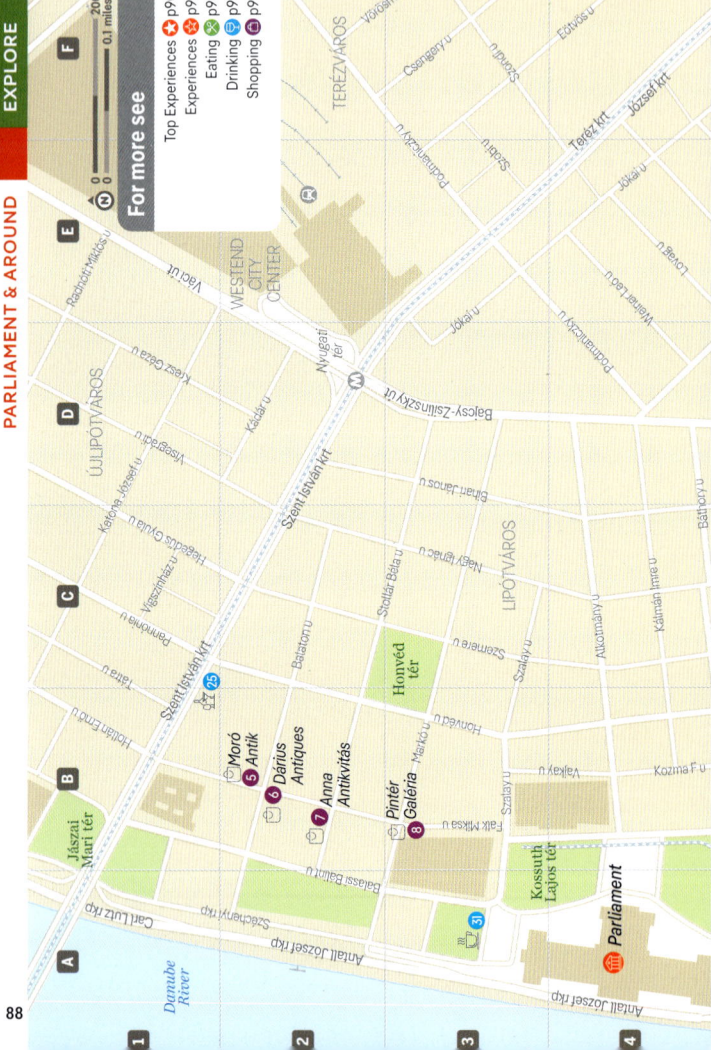

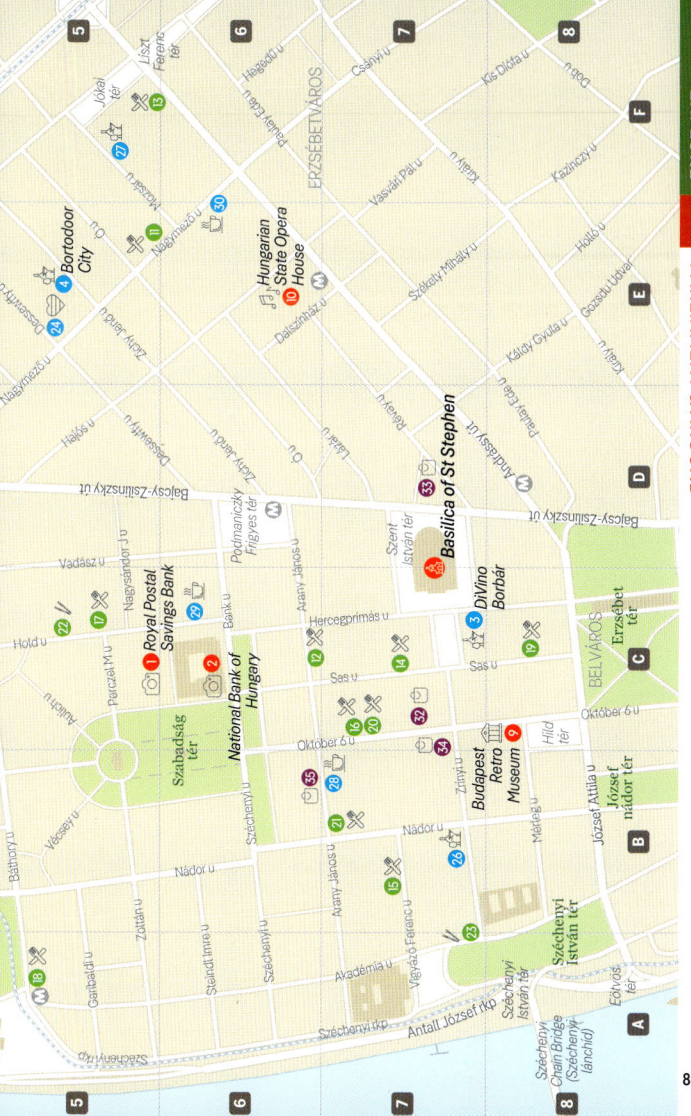

★ TOP EXPERIENCE

Parliament

Hungary's largest building stretches for 268m along the Danube in Pest. It's a vast, stately building, a repository of national treasures and a symbolic counterweight to the Royal Palace on Buda Hill across the river. The idea behind its placement was that the nation's future lay with popular democracy and not royal prerogative.

MAP: P88 **A4**

PLANNING TIP
Book ahead through Jegymester (*jegymester.hu*). Tours are usually by audio guide and available in 26 languages, including English. EU citizens pay half the standard adult/concession admission fee.

Scan for opening hours and to book ahead.

Parliament's Exterior

Designed by Imre Steindl in 1885 and completed just weeks before his death in 1902, this iconic structure's inspiration is thought to have been London's rebuilt Palace of Westminster, which opened in 1860. The building is a blend of many architectural styles (neo-Gothic, neo-Romanesque, neo-Baroque). Some 90 sculptures of the great and the good – kings, princes and historical figures – gaze out onto the Danube from the west facade, while the main door – the Lion Gate – gives on to revamped Kossuth Lajos tér, which has a state-of-the-art visitor centre on its northern side.

A Look Inside

You'll only see a handful of the building's 700 rooms on a guided tour. From the visitor centre, you ascend the 132 steps of the highly decorated Golden Staircase (there's a lift option) with sumptuous ceiling frescoes by Károly Lotz and stained glass by Miksa Roth. Next is the centrepiece: the 16-sided, 66m-high Dome Hall where the Crown of St Stephen, the nation's most important symbol, is on display, along with the 15th-century ceremonial sword, an orb (1301) and a 10th-century Persian-made sceptre. The sweeping 96-step Grand Staircase descends to the Lion Gate, but you'll move on to the vaulted

SSSANCHEZ/SHUTTERSTOCK ©

Debating Chamber with three dozen statues of traditional tradespeople and the 400-seat Congress Hall, where the upper house of the one-time bicameral assembly sat until 1944. It's almost identical to the National Assembly Hall, where parliamentary sessions are held in the South Wing.

Crown of St Stephen

The two-part crown, with its bent cross, pendants hanging on either side and enamelled plaques of the Apostles on the band, dates from the late 12th century and has become the symbol of the Hungarian nation. The crown has disappeared several times over the centuries – purloined or otherwise – only to reappear later. After WWII, it fell into the hands of the US army and was transferred to Fort Knox in Kentucky. It was only returned to Hungary in 1978.

QUICK BREAK
Facing Parliament to the south, **Pick Bistro & Deli** (p98) is a great Hungarian-style eatery where you can try the most famous salami in the country.

★ **TOP EXPERIENCE**

Basilica of St Stephen

This basilica is the most sacred Catholic church in Hungary, if for no other reason than that it contains the nation's most revered relic: the mummified right hand of the church's patron, King St Stephen. It was built over half a century, completed in 1905.

MAP: P88 **D7**

PLANNING TIP
Buy tickets online to avoid the queues at the ticket office, which is on the square just south of the basilica. Tickets are available to the basilica, the treasury, the dome and to all three.

Scan for opening hours and to book ahead.

The Dome

The basilica's facade is anchored by two hefty towers; the southwest one contains a bell weighing 9.25 tonnes. Behind the towers is the 96m-high dome, with statues of the four Evangelists filling its niches. It offers one of the best views in the city. If you want to climb all the way to the top, you'll face 302 steps. Otherwise take the normal-sized lift to the 3rd floor and walk 145 steps to the dome's exterior. If you can manage to get space in the second four-person lift on the 3rd floor, you'll only have to walk 28 steps from where the lift deposits you.

The Basilica's Nave

The interior glimmers in low-lit splendour, with Károly Lotz's golden mosaics on the inside of the dome seeming to produce a light all of their own. Noteworthy items include Alajos Stróbl's statue of the king-saint on the main altar and Gyula Benczúr's painting of St Stephen dedicating Hungary to the Virgin Mary and Christ Child, to the right in the north aisle. Below that painting is a glass case containing the basilica's major drawcard – the Holy Dexter (or Holy Right), the mummified right hand of St Stephen, an object of

POSZTOS/SHUTTERSTOCK ©

great devotion here. It was restored to Hungary by Habsburg empress Maria Theresa in 1771 after being discovered in a Bosnian monastery.

The Treasury

The 2nd floor contains a treasury of ecclesiastical objects, including censers, chalices, ciboria, croziers and vestments. Don't miss the Art Deco double monstrance (1938). Otherwise, the treasury is a veritable shine to Cardinal József Mindszenty, once a thorn in the side of the communist government, including his clothing, devotional objects and death mask.

QUICK BREAK
Café Kör (p98), a short walk from the basilica, is a long-standing favourite for lunch or a light meal at any time of day.

Walk the Triangle of Squares

This neighbourhood contains arguably Budapest's two most emblematic sites, Parliament and the Basilica of St Stephen, both among its most beautiful buildings. It also encompasses three very important squares that are masterpieces of engineering and help frame some of the city's best and most diverse architecture.

START	END	LENGTH
Széchenyi tér	Kossuth Lajos tér	1.6km; two hours

1 Meet Two Great Men

Begin your walk in **Széchenyi tér**, named after the late US President Franklin Roosevelt for more than a half-century, but now recalling the statesman who founded the **Hungarian Academy of Sciences** on the north side. On the east is the sumptuous Art Nouveau **Gresham Palace** (p121; 1907), now a luxury hotel. To the south is a statue of **Ferenc Deák**, who helped bring about the dual monarchy of Austria and Hungary in 1867. Below him is a well-coiffed Austrian boy, while the Hungarian kid's hair is tussled.

2 Heart of the District

Walk east to **Október 6 utca**, which is the centre of the neighbourhood. Here you'll find the erstwhile headquarters of the Central European University (now based in Vienna) and the lion's share of the district's restaurants, bars and cafes.

3 Odd Monuments

Continue north to **Szabadság tér** (Liberty Sq), which is filled with unusual monuments: a **Soviet Army memorial**, still sporting its wreathed hammer and sickle and topped with a large gold star; **statues** of the late US presidents Ronald Reagan and George H W Bush; and the controversial **Antifascist Monument** (2014), dedicated to the 'victims of the German occupation', which many find hypocritical. An alternative (and poignant) memorial of candles, letters and personal memorabilia has been set up by protesters.

4 Poignant Memorial

On the Danube embankment, to the west at the end of Zoltán utca, is the **Shoes on the Danube** memorial to Hungarian Jews shot and thrown into the river by members of the fascist Arrow Cross Party in 1944. It's a simple but poignant display of 60 pairs of old-style footwear in cast iron, set higgledy-piggledy along the riverbank.

5 New Lease of Life

The site of the Parliament, Budapest's most photographed building, riverside **Kossuth Lajos tér** has been restored to its original prewar design. Below it are two underground branches of the Museum of the Hungarian Parliament. 'In Memoriam: 25 October 1956' looks at the second night of the Uprising, when soldiers opened fire on a peaceful crowd, while the lapidarium has original sculptures and other stonework taken from the Parliament.

EXPERIENCES

Banking on Architecture   ARCHITECTURE

East of Szabadság tér is one of Pest's most beautiful buildings: the former **Royal Postal Savings Bank** (MAP: ① P88 C5), a Secessionist extravaganza of tiles and folk motifs built by Ödön Lechner in 1901. Southeast is the seat of the **National Bank of Hungary** (MAP: ② P88 C6). It has terracotta reliefs on all four sides that illustrate trade and commerce through history: Arab camel traders, African rug merchants, Egyptian grain farmers, Chinese tea salesmen and the inevitable solicitor witnessing contracts.

Taste Wine Expertly   WINE TASTING

Wine is very much part of the social scene in Budapest, and prices are usually quite reasonable. Old-fashioned wine bars ladle it out by the deci (decilitre, or 100mL), but if you're serious about wine, you should visit one of the Parliament area's excellent wine bars, where staff will offer recommendations. Near the basilica, **DiVino Borbár** (MAP: ③ P88 C7; *divinoborbar.hu*) is where wine tasting first became the obsession it is today. Choose from more than 150 options produced by some three-dozen young winemakers. Just off Nagymező utca, popular **Bortodoor City** (MAP: ④ P88 E5; *bortodoor.com*) is always fun and festive – a kind of 'wine pub' – but the owners take their ever-changing wine list seriously.

Searching for Old Stuff   ANTIQUING

While away a Saturday morning along Falk Miksa utca, which is lined with antique and curio shops and galleries. Start at **Moró Antik** (MAP: ⑤ P88 B2; *moroantik.hu*), with its considerable collection of antique swords and pistols, as well as

FAVOURITE HUNGARIAN WINES
Péter Lengyel is an omnivorous freelance translator, oenophile, wine consultant and restaurant reviewer.
Szászi's Kéknyelű (Badacsony) Made from a rare grape confined to Badacsony Hill on the northern shore of Lake Balaton, this white boasts a beguiling but subdued floral bouquet.
István Szepsy's Szent Tamás Furmint (Tokaj) Harvested from the finest vineyard for dry Furmint, this is an intense, expressive but sophisticated white.
Ruppert's Rosé (Villány) Crisp, vinous and dry; a classic onion-skin-colour rosé.
Tiffán's Grande Selection (Villány) A Bordeaux-style blend that plays with the French big ones; profound, concentrated and resonant.
István Szepsy's 6-puttonyos Aszú (Tokaj) Hungary's pre-eminent 'noble rot' offering from the undisputed leader in Tokaj. Massively sweet but balanced expertly by firm acidity.

porcelain, paintings and items from Asia. Opposite is **Dárius Antiques** (MAP: ❻ P88 **B2**; *dariusantik.hu*), with furniture, paintings, glass, porcelain, clocks and weapons. **Anna Antikvitás** (MAP: ❼ P88 **B2**; *annaantikvitas.hu*) specialises in folksy embroidered antique tablecloths, bed linen and some folk costumes. At the end of the road is **Pintér Galéria** (MAP: ❽ P88 **B3**; *pinteraukcioshaz.hu*), with a 2000-sq-metre showroom spread across a series of cellars. Pintér has everything, from furniture and chandeliers to oil paintings and chinaware.

Travel Back to the Bad Old Days
INTERACTIVE MUSEUM

MAP: ❾ P88 **C8**

The **Budapest Retro Museum** *(bpretro.com; adult/concession 5500/4500Ft)* travels back to Hungary between the 1950s and 1989. Here you can get behind the wheel of a police Lada, visit typical shops of the day (including a dated appliance store), sit in on an official news broadcast from a modern television studio, make a call from a pay telephone and experience a typical Budapest home, complete with the inevitable orange kitchen furnishings. It might feel a bit hokey at times, but the museum does bring forward a past that was really not that long ago and it's all very hands-on.

Visiting the Opera
CONCERT HALL

MAP: ❿ P88 **E6**

The neo-Renaissance **Hungarian State Opera House** *(opera.hu)* was completed in 1884 and is among the most beautiful buildings in Budapest, especially after its recent five-year restoration. It's worth a visit as much to admire the incredibly rich decoration inside as to view a performance and hear the perfect acoustics – the best in Europe. If you can't attend a performance, join one of the three one-hour daily tours in English (9000Ft), which include a 10-minute performance at the end.

MAGYAR THROUGH & THROUGH

Hungarians have made impressive contributions across a number of artistic fields – from cinema to fine arts – especially when you consider the nation's relatively small population.

Brassaï (Halász Gyula; 1899–1984) Known for his dramatic photographs of Paris at night.

George Cukor (1899–1983) American film producer and director.

Tony Curtis (Bernard Schwartz; 1925–2010) Perennial American actor.

Joe Eszterhas (1944–) American scriptwriter.

Harry Houdini (Erik Weisz; 1874–1926) Celebrated escape artist.

Bela Lugosi (Blaskó Béla; 1884–1956) Cinema's one and only Dracula.

Ernő Rubik (1944–) Inventor of the iconic cube-shaped puzzle.

LISTINGS

Best Places for...

⊖ Budget **⊖⊖** Midrange **⊖⊖⊖** Top End

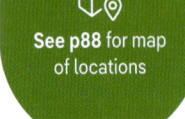
See p88 for map of locations

Eating

Top Picks in Lipótváros & Terézváros

Pizzica ⊖
 E5

If there's a finer pizza in all of Budapest, we don't know where to find it. *11am-11pm Mon-Thu, to midnight Fri & Sat*

Smokey Monkies ⊖
12 C6

If you like smokehouse eateries as much as we do, you'll beat a path to this place for its barbecued sandwiches and ribs. *11.30am-10pm Mon-Sat, to 9pm Sun*

Bigfish ⊖⊖
13 F5

Super-fresh fish and shellfish you can select yourself from the ice trays and then decide how you want it prepared. *noon-10pm*

Café Kör ⊖⊖
 C7

The 'Circle Café' is a long-standing favourite for lunch or dinner, but a great place for a light meal at any time. *noon-10pm Mon-Sat*

Mák ⊖⊖⊖
 B7

'Poppy' offers several inventive tasting menus of dishes and ingredients sourced in the Carpathian Basin that lean in Hungary's direction. *noon-2pm Sat, 6-11pm Wed-Sat*

Hungarian

Kisharang ⊖
16 C7

This miniature *étkezde* (diner) serves some of the best and most affordable Hungarian dishes in town. *11.30am-10pm*

Kispiac Bisztró ⊖⊖
 C5

Intimate, retro-style restaurant that prepares hearty fare such as wild-boar spare ribs and roast piglet. *noon-10pm Tue-Sat*

Pick Bistro & Deli ⊖⊖
 A5

Hungarian-style bistro and deli opposite Parliament where you can try the most famous salami in the country. *11.30am-11pm Mon-Sat, to 8pm Sun*

Borkonyha ⊖⊖⊖
19 C8

Michelin-starred restaurant with a contemporary approach to Hungarian cuisine; more than 100 different wines available. *6pm-midnight Mon-Fri, noon-midnight Sat*

Asian

Bombay Budapest ⊖⊖
 C7

This sleek and authentic Indian eatery has a wide range of curries and vegetarian offerings. *11.30am-4pm & 6pm-midnight*

Opium ⊖⊖
 B7

Enormous pan-Asian restaurant and bar serving a hybrid cuisine that mixes Vietnamese with Chinese and French. *11.30am-11pm*

Jin Galbi ⊖⊖⊖
 C5

Serves arguably the best Korean barbecue and has the greatest selection of *banchan* (side dishes) in Budapest. *11am-2.30pm & 5-9.30pm Mon-Sat*

Tokio Budapest ✪✪✪
23 A7

As authentic a Japanese eatery as you'll find outside of Nihon, with all the izakaya favourites and prices to match. *noon-midnight*

Drinking

Best Party Places
Alterego
24 E5

Budapest's top gay club, with a chic crowd, great music and inspired drag shows. *10pm-5am Fri, to 6am Sat*

Morrison's 2
25 C1

Still the biggest party venue in town; seven dance floors and just as many bars attract a mostly younger crowd. *5pm-6am*

Ötkert
26 B7

This daytime *lángos* (deep-fried dough with toppings) joint transforms into a popular three-floor dance club from Thursday into the weekend. *11am-5am Mon & Wed-Sat*

Kaledonia
27 F5

This expat bar lures in the crowds with 150-plus types of whisky and big-screen sports coverage. *2pm-midnight Mon-Fri, noon-midnight Sat & Sun*

Cafes
Espresso Embassy
28 B7

Some people say this upbeat cafe has the best espressos, flat whites, cappuccinos and lattes in town. *7am-5pm Mon-Fri, from 8am Sat & Sun*

Artizán
29 C6

This wonderful modern cafe serves wholefoods with no additives, shop-made sourdough bread and superb coffee. *7am-6pm Mon-Fri, 7.30am-1.30pm Sat*

Mai Manó Cafe
30 E6

This atmospheric cafe in the eponymous 1894 Art Nouveau building on Budapest's Broadway is perfect for people watching. *8am-midnight Sun-Thu, to 1am Fri & Sat*

Smúz Cafe
31 A3

We love the vibe at this cafe and bar with spectacular views of Parliament and the Danube, but we love its name (Schmooze) best. *10am-9pm Sun-Thu, to 10pm Fri & Sat*

Shopping

Books & Music
Bestsellers
32 C7

Top dog among English-language bookshops, with helpful staff. *9am-6.30pm Mon-Fri, 11am-6pm Sat, noon-6pm Sun*

Wave Music
33 D7

Cubbyhole shop, packed to the rafters with alternative LPs; it's an excellent outlet for indie guitar music. *11am-7pm Mon-Fri, to 5pm Sat*

Folk Art & Souvenirs
Memories of Hungary
34 C7

Located just west of the basilica, this branch of a chain shop has a good selection of mostly genuine handicrafts. *10am-10pm*

Originart Galéria
35 B6

Playful Hungarian handicrafts guaranteed to put a smile on your face, and with kiddie appeal too. *10am-6pm Mon-Fri*

Explore
Margaret Island & Northern Pest

Neither Buda nor Pest, leafy Margaret Island (Margit-sziget) sits in the middle of the Danube. Just 2.5km long, it's not graced with major sights, but you can easily spend half a day exploring its swimming complexes, thermal spa, gardens and centuries-old ruins – on a hot summer day, it offers a lovely escape. Cars are allowed on the island only as far as the hotels at the northern end.

The area to the island's east is called Újlipótváros (New Leopold Town) to distinguish it from Lipótváros (Leopold Town). It's a wonderful neighbourhood with tree-lined streets, boutiques, cafes and restaurants.

Getting Around

 Bus
Bus 26 covers the length of Margaret Island, running between Nyugati train station and Árpád Bridge. Bus 15 runs through Újlipótváros as it makes its way between Belváros and northern Pest.

 Tram
Trams 4 and 6 run along the southern end of both districts, which can be reached from the Inner Town on trams 2, 2B or 23.

🚎 **Trolleybus**
Trolleybuses 75 and especially 76 are excellent for Újlipótváros.

 Metro
The eastern end of Újlipótváros is best reached by metro (M3 Nyugati pályaudvar).

Margaret Bridge (p107), Margaret Island
ALEXEY OBLOV/SHUTTERSTOCK ©

THE BEST

HISTORICAL RUINS
Dominican convent (p106)

PLUNGE Palatinus Strand (p103)

TRAIN-SPOTTING Hungarian Railway History Park (p107)

FLIPPING FUN Pinball Museum (p107)

LATE-NIGHT MUSIC
Budapest Jazz Club (p107)

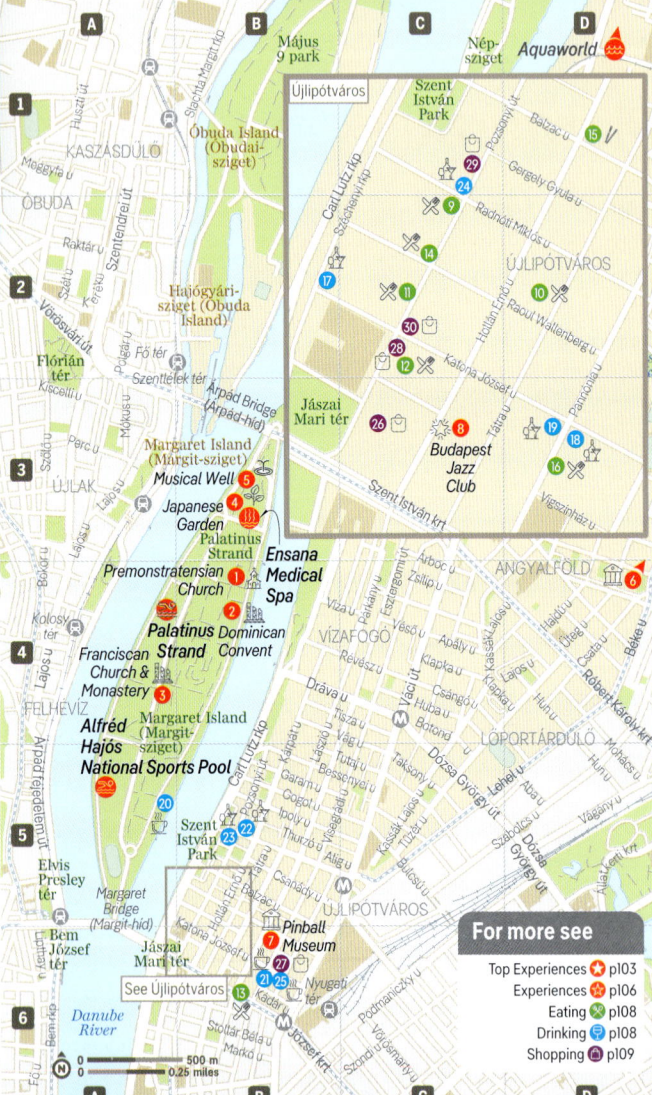

★ **TOP EXPERIENCE**

Diving in on Margaret Island

If you fancy taking a plunge, Margaret Island is just the place to do it – whether it be swimming laps in an Olympic-size pool where Olympians train, splashing around in Budapest's largest swimming complex, or relaxing in its most modern spa.

Doing Laps
The **Alfréd Hajós National Sports Pool** *(nsu.hu/letesitmeny/hajos-alfred-nemzeti-sportuszoda; adult/concession from 2500/1700Ft)* contains eight indoor and outdoor pools open to the public at various times of the day and week. Further north, on the west side of Margaret Island, is **Palatinus Strand** *(adult/child from 5000/3900Ft)* with 11 pools (two with thermal water), wave machines and water slides. This is the best place to bring the kids in summer and, with four of the pools covered, it stays open year-round.

Thermal Spa
Close to the island's northern end, the **Ensana Medical Spa** *(ensanahotels.com; adult/concession 10,000/6000Ft)* is modern and spick-and-span. A daily ticket includes entry to the swimming pools, sauna and steam room. The list of available medical treatments is impressive.

Water Park
Still feeling like a fish out of water? Head for **Aquaworld** *(aqua-world.hu; adult/child from 7500/3800Ft),* one of Europe's largest water parks, in Pest's far north. It has an adventure centre covered by a 72m-high dome, pools with a dozen slides and an array of saunas to keep the whole family at play all year long. Reach it on tram 14 from Lehel tér, or on bus 30 from Keleti train station.

PLANNING TIPS

Almost all pools and baths are open to both sexes, so bring a bathing suit or be prepared to rent one. Sandals/flip-flops are useful on slippery surfaces.

Scan for more information on Palatinus Strand.

WALKING TOUR

Walk the Length of the Island

The best way to explore Margaret Island is by strolling its length, from Margaret to Árpád bridges. Start by walking or taking tram 4 or 6 to the middle of Margaret Bridge (stop: Margit-sziget/Margit-híd), from where the access road will lead you to the island.

START	END	LENGTH
Margaret Bridge	Árpád Bridge	2.5km; two-and-a-half hours

1 Birth of a City

In the flower-bed roundabout just ahead of Margaret Bridge, the hollowed-out, lozenge-shaped **Centenary Monument** was unveiled in 1973 to mark the 100th anniversary of the union of Buda, Pest and Óbuda. It was an entirely different era in Budapest in the 1970s, and the sculptor filled the split cone with all sorts of socialist and nationalist symbols. It's like a time capsule on display.

2 Water Dances

Behind the monument is the delightful **musical fountain** that puts on a dramatic display five times a day with jets 'dancing' to music and shooting up to 10m into the air. Catch the last show at 9pm, when the fountain is illuminated by hundreds of coloured lights.

3 Diving In

The first of the island's two popular swimming pools is the indoor/outdoor **Alfréd Hajós National Sports Pool** (p103), where the Hungarian Olympic swimming and water polo teams train. It's named after the Olympic swimming champion who won the 100m and 1200m freestyle events at the first modern Olympiad in 1896. The huge **Palatinus Strand** (p103) complex is to the north.

4 Church & Monastery

Between the two pools, you'll pass the tower and extended wall of the 13th-century **Franciscan church and monastery** (p106). Habsburg archduke Joseph built a summer residence here (long since demolished) when he inherited the island in 1867, and it was a hotel until after WWII.

5 Island Viewpoint

Rising to the north is the landmark, Secessionist-style **water tower** *(margitszigetiszinhaz.hu; adult/child 500/300Ft)*, erected in 1911. Climb the 152 steps to the top of the 57m octagonal structure for a 360-degree view of the island. Below it is a 3500-seat **open-air theatre** used for concerts and plays in summer.

6 Place of Pilgrimage

A few steps east are more ruins, including a former **Dominican convent** (p106) and the grave of St Margaret, which is something of a pilgrimage site. Further north is the reconstructed Romanesque **Premonstratensian church** (p106), dedicated to St Michael.

7 Garden with Music

Head west and walk through the delightfully landscaped **Japanese Garden** (p106) to find the historic **Musical Well** (p106). From the stop nearby, southbound bus 26 will take you back to Margaret Bridge. Heading north, the same bus goes to the Göncz Árpád Városközpont metro station on the M3.

EXPERIENCES

Journey to the Middle Ages
RELIGIOUS RUINS

Margaret Island was always the domain of one religious order or another until the Turks arrived in the mid-16th century. They proceeded to turn what was then called the Island of Rabbits into – appropriately enough – a harem, from which all infidels were barred.

On the island's northeast side, the Romanesque **Premonstratensian church** (MAP: ① P102 B4), dedicated to St Michael by the order of White Canons, originally dates to the 12th century, though it was largely rebuilt in 1931. Just south are the ruins of the 13th-century **Dominican convent** (MAP: ② P102 B4), built by Béla IV, where his daughter, St Margaret, took the veil. It remained a working convent until the Ottoman occupation. Adjoining are the remains of a medieval palace.

To the southwest, almost in the island's centre, are the reconstructed ruins of a one-time **Franciscan church and monastery** (MAP: ③ P102 A4) that dates back to the late 13th century. Still visible in the western wall is a doorway leading to the organ loft, as well as a spiral staircase and fine arched window.

Enjoy Flowers Set to Music
GARDEN WITH MUSIC

At the northwestern end of Margaret Island, the **Japanese Garden** (MAP: ④ P102 B3) has ponds filled with koi fish and lily pads, as well as bamboo groves, miniature maples, dawn redwoods, cypresses, a small wooden bridge and a waterfall. Don't be surprised if you hear some rather incongruous music in the background, and even a few trumpet blasts emanating nearby. It's coming from the **Musical Well** (MAP: ⑤ P102 B3), which sits on a raised gazebo a few steps away. This is a replica of a 1936 fountain in Marosvásárhely (now Târgu Mureș) in Transylvania, and is topped with a statue of Neptune that revolves (in theory) in line with the sun. The

ST MARGARET: RESIDENT & NAMESAKE

Margaret Island's most famous resident was the eponymous Margaret (1242–71), the daughter of Béla IV. According to legend, the king pledged her to a nunnery in exchange for the expulsion of the Mongols, who had overrun Hungary in 1241. If we're to believe *The Lives of the Saints*, she enjoyed her life of devotion, especially the mortification-of-the-flesh parts. Canonised only in 1943, St Margaret commands something of a cult following in Hungary. Among the ruins of the Dominican convent, a red-marble sepulchre cover surrounded by a wrought-iron grille marks her original resting place.

structure plays Hungarian melodies every hour on the hour and a four-trombone ditty on the half-hour. At ground level, it earns the second part of its name: three taps pump out potable well water.

Do Some Historical Train-spotting
TRANSPORT MUSEUM

MAP: P102 D4

Though a bit out of the way from Újlipótváros – it's about 4.5km northeast of Lehel tér – the **Hungarian Railway History Park** (*vasuttortenetipark.hu; adult/child 2700/1200Ft*) will be irresistible to train-spotters. The largely outdoor museum claims to be Europe's largest open-air railway entertainment park, with 100 examples of locomotives and other rolling stock, plus an exhibition on the history of the railway in Hungary. There's a wonderful array of hands-on activities for kids, mostly involving getting behind the wheel. Riding the miniature locomotive is a real treat. Reach it on tram 14 from Lehel tér, or bus 30 or 30A from Keleti train station.

Flip till you Drop
INTERACTIVE MUSEUM

MAP: ⑦ P102 B6

Release your inner Elton John – with or without the 1.5m-high boots (see the 1975 film *Tommy*) – for the **Pinball Museum** (*flippermuzeum.hu; adult/concession 5000/3600Ft*) in Újlipótváros. Though rather specialised and quirky, this basement is home to some 160 vintage pinball machines and you can play all but the oldest wooden models, which date back as far as 1947. As the largest collection in Europe that's open to the public and interactive, it has quite a fan club.

Listen to All that Jazz
LIVE MUSIC

MAP: ⑧ P102 C3

The sophisticated **Budapest Jazz Club** (*bjc.hu*) is the place to go if you want to hear jazz, be it traditional, fusion, Latin or vocal. International and local performers take to the stage in the modern concert hall, which is equipped with a state-of-the-art sound system. Concerts take place most nights at 8pm, with jam sessions usually at 10pm from Tuesday to Saturday.

SPAN WITH A BEND
Margaret Bridge introduces the Big Ring Rd to Buda. It's unique in that it doglegs in the middle in order to stand at right angles to the Danube where it converges at the southern tip of Margaret Island. The bridge was built in 1876 as the second permanent bridge over the Danube in Budapest. The spur leading to the island was added in 1901. Like all the other spans across the Danube, Margaret Bridge was destroyed during WWII and only rebuilt in its aftermath. During reconstruction, much of the original steel was lifted from the river and incorporated into the new structure.

LISTINGS

Best Places for...

€ Budget €€ Midrange €€€ Top End

See p102 for map of locations

Eating

Hungarian

Pozsonyi Kisvendéglő €
9 C2

Visit this throwback restaurant for the ultimate local Budapest experience: gargantuan portions of Hungarian classics, rock-bottom prices and a cast of local characters. *9am-midnight Mon-Fri, from 10am Sat & Sun*

Firkász €€
10 D2

An unmissable 'nostalgia' spot thanks to the memorabilia on the walls, great homestyle dishes and soft piano music three nights a week. *noon-11pm*

Kiskakukk €€
11 C2

This ever-so-traditional Hungarian eatery with a retro shop sign in front has been serving up classic *gulyásleves* (hearty beef soup) and Jewish-style *sólet* (stew) with smoked goose for over a century. *noon-midnight*

Middle Eastern & Mediterranean

Babka €€
12 C2

Come for excellent meze and other Middle Eastern dishes, genuinely friendly service and a hip crowd. *5-11pm Mon, noon-11pm Tue, Wed & Sun, to midnight Thu-Sat*

Okay Italia €€
13 B6

This perennially popular place does a full range of dishes, but most people come for the imaginative pasta and pizza. *11am-11pm Mon-Fri, from 11.30am Sat & Sun*

UnoMas €€€
14 C2

A stylish new Iberian spot on 'the strip' offering authentic but pricey tapas, with particularly good seafood choices. *noon-midnight*

Asian

Oriental Soup House €
15 D1

This Vietnamese soup house is a relatively slick affair and has authentic pho and bun cha, including vegetarian versions. *11.30am-10pm Sun-Thu, to 11pm Fri & Sat*

Punjab Tandoori €
16 D3

The much expanded and brighter Punjab Tandoori still serves some of Budapest's best Indian food, especially the signature tandoori and vegetarian dishes. *noon-10pm Tue-Sun*

Drinking

Pubs & Bars

Gaby's
17 B2

The American-run, gay-friendly bar and restaurant on the Danube is just the ticket for a cocktail or three. *noon-11pm Sun-Thu, to midnight Fri & Sat*

Blue Tomato
 D3

This popular boozer is like something out of the classic American sitcom *Cheers*. *11am-midnight Mon-Wed, to 2am Thu, to 4am Fri & Sat, to 11pm Sun*

Mosselen
 D3

Bar/restaurant with a wide selection of Belgian beers, including eight on tap and 50 fruit-flavoured bottled brews. *noon-midnight*

Outdoor Drinks

Hippie Island
 A5

With peace signs and psychedelic colours everywhere, this throwback is a comfortable, mostly outdoor seasonal cafe on Margaret Island. *8.30am-midnight*

Figaró Kert
 B6

Seasonal bar and cafe that's an oasis in Újlipótváros' concrete jungle. *8.30am-10pm*

Sarki Fűszeres
 B5

This delightful, retro-style cafe in an Art Deco corner building is the perfect place for brunch, a late breakfast or a speciality coffee. Outside seating. *8am-6pm Mon, to 8pm Tue-Fri, 9am-5pm Sat, to 3pm Sun*

Cafes

Dunapark
 B5

Art Deco landmark, built as a cinema in 1938, that's a commendable lite-bite restaurant, doubling as a coffee-and-cake halt. *9am-9pm*

Babka Deli
 C1

This New York–style deli is also a great place to pop in to any time of the day for a coffee and something sweet. *9am-7pm Mon-Fri, to 6pm Sat & Sun*

Stranger Cafe
 B6

Unassuming but very welcoming cafe, away from the hubbub of Pozsony út. A great place for brunch or just a pit stop. *8am-7pm Mon-Fri, 10am-6pm Sat & Sun*

Shopping

Food & Drink

Mézes Kuckó
 C3

Come to the tiny 'Honey Nook' for nut-and-honey cookies, colourful heart-shaped *mézeskalácsok* (honey cakes) and several types of honey. *10am-6pm Mon-Fri, 9am-1pm Sat*

Ligeti Bolt
 B6

This 100% package-free shop sells pasta, nuts, jam, dairy and long-shelf-life products and kitchen accessories. *9am-7pm Mon-Fri, 10am-3pm Sat*

Zsebi
 C2

This cool bakery has a mouthwatering assortment of baked goods and shop-made jams, preserves and honey. *7.30am-5.30pm*

Fromage
 C1

Stacked high with cheeses, prepared meats and other picnic supplies perfect for an afternoon of snacking on Margaret Island. *7.30am-8pm Mon-Fri, 8.30am-7pm Sat*

Stühmer
 C2

Visit this sweet shop for its chocolate made in Hungary since 1868. *9am-7pm Mon-Sat*

See p125 for eating, drinking and shopping listings

Explore
Erzsébetváros & the Jewish Quarter

Located at Budapest's heart, Erzsébetváros is one of the city's most vibrant neighbourhoods, with deep historical roots, and you'll probably spend much of your time here. By day, it's a lovely place to wander, with cute cafes, vintage stores, random street art, great museums and plenty of evidence of the large Jewish community that has always been here. Come night, it turns into Budapest's party quarter, heaving with tourists and locals jumping between ruin bars, garden clubs, wineries and craft-beer bars. This is where the ruin-pub *(romkocsma)* phenomenon was born and continues to thrive.

Getting Around

Walking
The easiest way to get around Erzsébetváros is on foot.

E-scooter
Rent a Lime e-scooter through its app, but watch out for traffic in the narrow streets.

 **Tram 74**
Takes you from the Great Synagogue all the way to City Park.

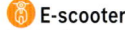 **M2**
Has several stops in the neighbourhood, including Astoria, Blaha Lujza tér and Keleti railway station.

 Tram 4-6
Travels from Erzsébet körút to Buda or the rest of Pest.

THE BEST

HISTORIC SIGHT Great Synagogue (p114)

MAJOR MUSEUM House of Terror (p115)

QUIRKY MUSEUM Liszt Ferenc Memorial Museum (p120)

HISTORIC CAFE New York Café (p120)

NIGHTLIFE SPOT Szimpla Kert (p124)

New York Café (p120)
JULIANO GALVAO GOMES/SHUTTERSTOCK ©

ERZSÉBETVÁROS & THE JEWISH QUARTER

EXPLORE

Map features:
- 9 Fasor Calvinist Church
- 8 Léderer House
- 7 (E2)
- Kodály körönd
- 3 Liszt Ferenc Memorial Museum
- House of Terror
- 6 Lindenbaum House
- 2 Nyugati Railway Station
- WESTEND CITY CENTER
- TERÉZVÁROS
- LIPÓTVÁROS
- ERZSÉBETVÁROS

For more see
- Top Experiences ★ p114
- Experiences ⊛ p120
- Eating ⊗ p125
- Drinking ⊙ p125
- Shopping ⊙ p125

112

ERZSÉBETVÁROS & THE JEWISH QUARTER

Map Labels

- Hevesi Sándor tér
- Almássy tér
- Szövetség u
- Alsóerdősor u
- Kiss József u
- Bezerédi u
- Népszínház u
- JÓZSEFVÁROS
- Csokonai u
- Osvát u
- New York Café
- József krt
- Blaha Lujza tér
- Somogyi B u
- Síp u
- Nyáry u
- Gyulai Pál u
- Rákóczi út
- Dohány u
- Kazinczy u
- Klauzál u
- Akácfa u
- Erzsébet krt
- Hársfa u
- Erzsébetváros Bilingual Elementary School
- Liszt Ferenc Academy of Music
- Kürt u
- Kertész u
- Dob u
- Csányi u
- Motivation is a Wonderland
- Beautify Budapest
- Füge Udvar
- Instant-Fogas
- Klauzál tér
- E-Exit
- Museum of Electrical Engineering Budapest
- CoXx
- Neverland
- Nagy Diófa u
- Köleves Kert
- Kis Diófa u
- Wesselényi u
- Szimpla Kert
- Great Synagogue
- Gozsdu Mission
- Rubik's Cube Mural
- Angel of Budapest
- Vasvári Pál u
- Holló u
- Gozsdu Courtyard
- Sissi
- Tuk Tuk Bar
- Andrássy út
- Király u
- Hegedű u
- Nagymező u
- Paulay Ede u
- Dalszínház u
- Révay u
- Madách Imre út
- Károly krt
- Asbóth u
- Semmelweis u
- Gerlóczy u
- Városház u
- Sütő u
- Deák Ferenc tér
- Erzsébet tér
- BELVÁROS
- Káldy Gyula u
- Bajcsy-Zsilinszky út
- Bank u
- Podmaniczky Frigyes tér
- Szent István tér
- Lázár u
- Ó u
- A, B, C, D, E, F
- 5, 6, 7, 8

113

★ **TOP EXPERIENCE**

Great Synagogue

With a red-and-yellow facade and two enormous Moorish-style towers, Budapest's stunning Great Synagogue is the largest Jewish house of worship in Europe. Visit for its majestic architecture, the Hungarian Jewish Museum and Archives and the mournful gardens centred by the Holocaust Tree of Life Memorial.

MAP: P112 **B8**

PLANNING TIP
Tickets include an informative 45-minute tour in eight languages. Find the flag corresponding to your language inside the synagogue and wait there for your guide – tours start every 30 to 60 minutes.

Scan for opening hours and tickets.

The 'Jewish Cathedral'
As the Great Synagogue was completed in 1859 for the Neolog Jewry – liberal, progressive and modernist Jews more inclined toward integration into Hungarian society since the Era of Emancipation in the 19th century – it has some distinctive Christian elements, including pulpits, a 5000-pipe organ and a central rose window. Don't miss the carvings on the Ark of the Covenant, and the wall and ceiling frescoes of multicoloured and gold geometric shapes.

Raoul Wallenberg Memorial Park
What was meant as a garden became the burial place for nearly 2600 Jewish people who perished during the Holocaust. The centrepiece is the Holocaust Tree of Life Memorial, a weeping willow made of iron, the leaves of which are engraved with the names of some of the victims. Nearby is a black-marble memorial to two-dozen 'Righteous Among the Nations'. Behind, a stained-glass memorial remembers Holocaust victims, while in front, a plaque commemorates Nicholas Winton, the 'British Schindler' portrayed by Anthony Hopkins in the 2023 film *One Life*.

Hungarian Jewish Museum & Archives
The upstairs annex contains interesting items related to both religious and everyday life, such as liturgical items in silver, manuscripts and a dozen stained-glass windows of Biblical scenes.

⭐ **TOP EXPERIENCE**

House of Terror

This moving museum focuses on the atrocities of Hungary's fascist and Stalinist regimes and commemorates their victims. The permanent exhibition is in the former headquarters of the Hungarian Nazis and, later, the Communist Secret Police, used for imprisoning, interrogating and torturing 'enemies of the state'.

MAP: P112 **D3**

A Disturbing Building
The walls of the headquarters of the Hungarian Nazi Arrow Cross Party, and later (from 1945–56) the Communist Secret Police (the ÁVÓ and its successor, the ÁVH) were allegedly of double thickness to muffle screams. On arrival, the facade displays photos of the many victims, while the (communist) star and the (fascist) pointed Greek cross at the entrance, and the massive tank in the central courtyard, make for a jarring introduction.

Descend into Darkness
Start by taking the lift to the top floor to walk though displays on pre- and post-WWII history and get a clearer picture of events leading up to the 1956 Uprising. Then descend into the exhibition's most harrowing area – the basement, a true realm of fear and pain.

'Don't Just Guard Them, Hate Them Too'
The ÁVÓ's motto creeps under your skin as you view the basement's reconstructed prison cells, where people were detained and horrifically tortured. The Hall of Tears is a solemn place to pay your respects, while looking into the eyes of spies, torturers and turncoats at the Perpetrators' Gallery on the staircase is especially chilling.

PLANNING TIP
Renting an audio guide is possible, while sheets of paper detailing what's on display are available in English in each room.

Scan this QR code for opening hours, tickets and more details.

WALKING TOUR

Walk Erzsébetváros & the Jewish Quarter

Inner Erzsébetváros has always been predominantly Jewish, home to three beautiful synagogues, and was also the site of the Budapest ghetto, where Jews were forced to live when the Nazis occupied Hungary in 1944. Discover the major sights of Jewish history, passing by random street art, cafes and restaurants.

START	END	LENGTH
Liszt Ferenc tér	Ghetto Wall Memorial	2.5km; one-and-a-half hours

1 In the Footsteps of Franz Liszt

Begin the walk in restaurant- and cafe-packed **Liszt Ferenc tér** (p120), viewing the statue of Liszt Ferenc and poking your head into the sumptuous **Liszt Ferenc Academy of Music** (p120), a university and concert hall in one.

2 Life of the Neolog Jewry

Head southwest along Király utca. You'll pass the **Church of St Teresa**, containing a massive Neoclassical altar designed in 1822. Look up directly opposite the church at Király utca 47 for an interesting neo-Gothic house built in 1847, with a delightful oriel window. Then turn onto Csányi utca, where you'll find **Csányi5** (p123), a museum showcasing the living quarters of a 19th-century Neolog Jewish family.

3 Synagogue with Art Nouveau Touches

Keep walking until you reach the heart of the old Jewish Quarter, **Klauzál tér**. A continued Jewish presence is evident in the surrounding streets and the many kosher restaurants around. Nearby is the **Kazinczy St Synagogue** with Art Nouveau elements and brightly coloured geometrical decorations throughout.

4 Sneak a Peek

Head back to Király utca, and if the gate at No 15 is open, walk to the courtyard's rear to see a 30m-long stretch of the original **ghetto wall**, rebuilt in 2010. Otherwise, just peer through the slit in the gate.

5 Cafes, Bars & Clubs

The next turn on the left is the passageway called **Gozsdu Courtyard** (p121), now the district's number-one nightlife destination lined with bars, cafes, clubs and restaurants.

6 A Stunning Synagogue

Continue on Dob utca to Rumbach Sebestyén utca. You'll pass by an unusual monument – a memorial to Swiss consul Carl Lutz, who, like Raoul Wallenberg, provided Jews with false papers in 1944. Before you reach the **Rumbach Street Synagogue**, with its red, blue and gold interior symbolising the heart, the intellect and wealth, note two major **murals** (p122).

7 Europe's Largest Synagogue

Turn around and head to the **Great Synagogue** (p114), Europe's largest Jewish house of worship. Don't miss visiting the garden called Raoul Wallenberg Memorial Park.

8 The Old Jewish Quarter

Follow Dohány utca until you reach the **Ghetto Wall Memorial**, featuring a map of the old Jewish Quarter with small holes to peer through to view historical scenes, plus religious verses and a summary of Jewish life in Budapest.

WALKING TOUR

Hunt for Guerilla Statues

Hungarian-Ukrainian guerilla artist Mihály Kolodko deposits cute, commemorative, thought-provoking and often funny bronze statuettes all around Budapest. Follow our walking tour to find some of his best ones, but keep your eyes peeled as not all of them are immediately obvious.

START	END	LENGTH
Great Synagogue	City Park	3.5km; two hours

1 Meet Tivadar Herzl
Start at the **Great Synagogue** (p114), where on a lamppost outside you'll find a **statuette of Tivadar Herzl**, the father of modern political Zionism.

2 The Writer of 'Gloomy Sunday'
Follow Wesselényi utca until you reach Akácfa utca. At No 38, find **Rezső Seress**, the writer of Hungary's 'suicide song', *Gloomy Sunday*, on the building's facade.

3 Legendary Keys
Outside the **New York Café** (p120), you'll find a **diver** retrieving the cafe's keys from the Danube. Rumour has it that on its opening night in 1894, author Ferenc Molnár and his journalist friends threw the keys of the coffeehouse into the Danube so that it could never close. This might have actually happened in 1927 when the cafe reopened after WWI (as Molnár was only 16 in 1894), but it's a significant event that has since been symbolically repeated more than once with a fake key.

4 An Alfa Romeo
Hevesi Sándor tér is home to the not-so-mini **Fourteen-carat Car**, an Alfa Romeo that honours Hungarian writer Jenő Rejtő.

5 A Hungarian Hero
At Rózsa utca 36, find the statuette of **Hanna Szenes**, one of 37 Jewish SOE recruits (agents conducting espionage, sabotage and reconnaissance in German-occupied Europe) who were parachuted into Yugoslavia to prevent the deportation of Hungarian Jews in 1944.

6 Take a Peek
Look inside **Noah's Ark** on Bethlen Gábor tér to see rainbow-coloured windows evoking the essential Bible story.

7 The Laziest Cat
Find **Garfield** – the only colourful Kolodko statue, created in 2023 to celebrate the 45th birthday of the iconic character – on the back fence of Budapest's Veterinary University on Dembinszky utca.

8 Winnie the Pooh & Beyond
On the facade of Damjanich utca 27, you'll find **Winnie The Pooh** holding an empty honey pot, honouring Hungarian author Frigyes Karinthy, who translated Milne's beloved tale into Hungarian and was born in this house. Nearby on Nefelejcs utca, inside the **Miksa Róth Memorial House** (p121), a pocket-sized **Róth** is planning his next masterpiece under a lamp, while within **City Park** (p138), you'll find **Drakula** (p28) – more precisely, Hungarian actor Béla Lugosi, famed for his sinister portrayal of Count Dracula – reading behind **Vajdahunyad Castle** (p138), and a **skateboard with boots and bones** sticking out of them by the **Museum of Ethnography** (p141).

EXPERIENCES

Marvel at the New York Café
CAFE

MAP: ① P112 E7

An ever-present long queue outside the **New York Café** *(newyork cafe.hu)* will certainly catch your eye when in Erzsébetváros. Once voted the world's most beautiful coffeehouse, the historic hangout is on the bucket list of many travellers. Inside, immerse yourself in authentic 19th-century coffeehouse culture amid gilded and marble surfaces, etched glass, frescoes and flowers, while live Hungarian music imbues the aristocratic atmosphere. During Hungary's Belle Époque, the cafe was a haunt for the country's literary greats and the birthplace of many outstanding books, poems and papers.

Tour the Liszt Ferenc Academy of Music
ACADEMY AND CONCERT HALL

MAP: ② P112 D5

Opened in 1875, the **Liszt Ferenc Academy of Music** *(zeneaka demia.hu)* is the only university in the world founded by Franz Liszt. Today, it's housed in a 1907 Art Nouveau building and doubles as Budapest's top classical-music venue. The renovated interior, which has two concert halls and is richly embellished with Zsolnay porcelain and frescoes, is worth visiting on a guided tour (*5300Ft*) if you're not attending a performance. Near the academy on Liszt Ferenc tér, a statue commemorates the great composer.

Visit the Liszt Ferenc Memorial Museum
MUSEUM

MAP: ③ P112 D3

A wonderful little **museum** *(lisztmuseum.hu; adult/student 3000/1500Ft)* is housed in the Old Music Academy where the great composer Franz Liszt lived in a 1st-floor apartment for five years until his death in 1886. The rooms are filled with his pianos (including a tiny glass one) and personal effects – all original.

🎵 **MUSIC'S FIRST SUPERSTAR**

Young people shrieking, screaming and swooning at the sight of their music idols is nothing new. But would you have thought this phenomenon started in the classical concert halls of 19th-century Europe? 'Lisztomania' was a term coined by German poet and Franz Liszt's contemporary, Heinrich Heine, who noted that 'women tore at each other's hair in trying to lay hands on a glass or handkerchief that Liszt had used'. One of the greatest pianists that ever lived was a true performer, tossing his shoulder-length locks and swaying hypnotically over the keyboard as he played, completely captivating his often hysterical audiences.

Guzzle Drinks at Gozsdu Courtyard
NIGHTLIFE

MAP: ④ P112 B7

Erzsébetváros has Budapest's most exciting nightlife, and **Gozsdu Courtyard** is its heart. It's a continuous 'courtyard' running a few hundred metres between Király utca and Dob utca. A residential complex of seven blocks and six interconnecting courtyards when it was built in 1901, and part of the Jewish Ghetto during WWII, it's now lined with bars, clubs, cafes and restaurants, and pulses with music and merrymakers from dusk to dawn.

Explore the Miksa Róth Memorial House
MUSEUM

MAP: ⑤ P112 F6

Many Budapest buildings from the belle époque, such as the Parliament, Széchenyi Baths, Gresham Palace and scores of private mansions, would simply not look the same without one man – renowned stained-glass and mosaic artist Miksa Róth, who even left his mark on the cupola of Mexico City's Palace of Fine Arts. A great **museum** *(rothmuzeum.hu; adult/student 1000/500Ft)* on Nefelejcs utca, not far from City Park, exhibits the works of the Art Nouveau artist over two floors of the apartment and studio where he lived and worked from 1911 until his death. The 1st floor still looks the same as the Róth family left it, giving visitors an insight into the living quarters of a 20th-century middle-class Hungarian family. Downstairs, an array of Róth's outstanding glass and mosaic art is on display, including *Pax*, winner of a silver medal at the Paris World Exhibition in 1900, and a flabbergasting Art Nouveau fireplace.

Admire Art Nouveau Buildings
NOTABLE BUILDINGS

Erzsébetváros has a number of schools, churches and private homes that are exceptional examples of Art Nouveau and worth an admiring glance. Designed by Frigyes Spiegel in 1896 as the city's first Art Nouveau block, the entire front elevation of **Lindenbaum House** (MAP: ⑥ P112 C2; *Izabella utca 94*) is covered with suns, stars, peacocks, flowers, snakes, foxes and long-tressed nudes. The two women sculptures framing the main door of **Sonnenberg House** (MAP: ⑦ P112 E1; *Munkácsy Mihály utca 23*) are rare. **Léderer House** (MAP: ⑧ P112 E1; *VI Bajza utca 42*) has lovely mosaics under the main ledge. The **Fasor Calvinist Church** (MAP: ⑨ P112 F3; *VII Városligeti fasor 7*) is an amazing example of late Art Nouveau (1913), with carved wooden gates, stained glass and ceramic tiles. Finally, don't miss the **Erzsébetváros Bilingual Elementary School** (MAP: ⑩ P112 E5; *VII Dob utca 85*), with front-elevation mosaics on its facade.

Walk along Andrássy út   AVENUE
MAP: **11** P112 **B5**

Starting at Deák Ferenc tér and ending at Heroes' Square and the sprawling City Park, the UNESCO World Heritage–listed **Andrássy út** is a tree-lined parade of knock-out architecture, best enjoyed as a long stroll from the Hungarian State Opera House to the park. If you prefer a speedier journey, take the charmingly retro Millennium Underground, the oldest metro line in continental Europe.

Enjoy Escape Games   ESCAPE ROOMS

The door closes behind your back, the clock starts ticking. You race to solve real-life riddles and mind-boggling puzzles in order to get out. Tricky clues keep coming your way to help crack the code that will finally set you free. Sounds fun? Budapest is the undisputed European capital of live escape games, and the themes, designs and concepts of rooms are endless, from sinister scenes of claustrophobic nightmares to venues of visually pleasing puzzles. In Erzsébetváros, **Neverland** (MAP: **12** P112 **C8**; *neverland.hu*), **Gozsdu Mission** (MAP: **13** P112 **B7**; *gozsdumission.hu*) and **E-Exit** (MAP: **14** P112 **D7**; *escaperoom.hu*) are worth a try.

Stumble upon Street Art   MURALS

One great thing about walking around Erzsébetváros is chancing upon stunning painted murals on firewalls. Some of the best include **Beautify Budapest** (MAP: **15** P112 **D7**; *Akácfa utca 27*), a fun depiction of summer essentials in the capital. **Angel of Budapest** (MAP: **16** P112 **B8**) under Dob utca 4 portrays Spanish diplomat Ángel Sanz Briz, credited with having saved more than 5000 Hungarian Jews from the Holocaust in 1944. **Motivation is a Wonderland** (MAP: **17** P112 **D6**; *Kertész utca 27*) borrows its theme from *Alice's Adventures in Wonderland*. Rumbach Sebestyén utca is home to three murals: **Rubik's Cube** (MAP: **18** P112 **B7**) commemorates the iconic Hungarian

---

STUMBLING STONES

Roaming the streets of Budapest, you'll stumble upon tiny brass plaques embedded in the pavement. These are called Stolpersteine, or stumbling stones, and were created by German artist Gunter Demnig as part of the world's largest decentralised memorial to Holocaust victims. Each one commemorates a person beside their last-known location, with inscriptions of their name, date of birth and fate – suicide, exile or, in the majority of cases, deportation and extermination. Once you know they're there, you'll see them everywhere, but mostly in Erzsébetváros and, as the artist himself once said: 'You won't fall, but if you stumble and look, you must bow down with your head and your heart.'

invention; **6:3** (MAP: 19 P112 **B7**) immortalises the football match when the nation's Golden Team with Ferenc Puskás defeated England 6–3 at Wembley Stadium; and **Sissi** (MAP: 20 P112 **B7**) features Hungary's favourite Queen, after whom the district was named – it's also a love letter to the neighbourhood.

Explore Nyugati Railway Station   RAILWAY STATION
MAP: 21 P112 **B2**

The large iron-and-glass **Nyugati Railway Station** was built in 1877 by the Paris-based Eiffel Company. It was totally destroyed in WWII, but rebuilt in 1945. One of its most famous events was when a train carriage crashed through the enormous glass screen on the main facade in 1962, coming to rest on the pavement outside. Thankfully, staff were quick to issue warnings over the loudspeakers, so only one person was injured. The old dining hall on the station's south side has housed one of the world's most elegant McDonald's since the 1980s. To the north is WestEnd, a shopping centre that was once the largest in central Europe.

Tour Csányi5   MUSEUM
MAP: 22 P112 **C6**

The permanent exhibition at this two-storey **residential building** (erzsitt.hu; adult/student 2500/1500Ft) features reconstructed rooms presenting the life of Pest's Neolog Jewry from a time of societal inclusion at the end of the 19th century to a time of exclusion in 1945. Walk around the home of a well-to-do family, visit the office of a rabbi, the workshop of a seamstress or the simple studio of a poor worker.

See Lotz Frescoes at Keleti Railway Station   RAILWAY STATION
MAP: 23 P112 **F7**

A key spot for international train travel, **Keleti (Eastern) Railway Station** is not only Budapest's busiest transport hub, but also an architectural gem blending neo-Renaissance and eclectic styles. Keleti is worth a visit for its Lotz Hall alone, with its walls festooned with murals by renowned Romanticist painters Mór Thán and Károly Lotz.

Discover the District's Gay Side   LGBTIQ+ BARS

In a city with such a bustling nightlife, Budapest's gay bar scene is not as large as you might expect. But as we all know, size isn't everything and the half-dozen-or-so LGBTIQ+ bars, cafes and clubs cater to most needs. In Erzsébetváros, **Habroló** (MAP: 24 P112 **C8**; habrolo.hu) is a small and welcoming cafe and bar on two levels. Around the corner and beckoning to the daring is **CoXx** (MAP: 25 P112 **D8**; coxx.hu), the city's only gay cruise club. Much more subdued and a 10-minute walk north is the **Tuk Tuk Bar** (MAP: 26 P112 **B6**;

tuktukbar.hu), with ever-so-Asian-inspired design.

Visit the Museum of Electrical Engineering Budapest MUSEUM

MAP: 27 P112 C7

Though this **museum** *(kozlekedesimuzeum.hu; adult/student 1600/800Ft)* might not sound like everyone's cup of tea, some of the exhibits inside the Bauhaus-style building are unusual enough to warrant a visit. If you've ever wondered how the communist-era alarm system on the barbed-wire fence that separated Hungary and Austria functioned, this is your spot. There are tonnes of old household appliances (many still work) and colourful communist-era neon shop signs adorn the outside courtyard. The weirdest display is the collection – one of the largest in the world – of electricity-consumption meters, which includes one installed in the apartment of 'Rákosi Mátyás elvtárs' (Comrade Mátyás Rákosi), the Communist Party secretary, on his 60th birthday in 1952, and another recalling Stalin's 70th birthday in 1948.

Booze at Ruin Bars NIGHTLIFE

Take an empty, rundown residential building, stuff it with furniture found in skips and random knick-knacks, set up a bar counter and perhaps a corner for DJ decks and voilá – your ruin bar *(romkocsma)* is ready. Erzsébetváros is ruin-bar central, where bare-brick venues are a dime-a-dozen along the Grand Boulevard. The granddaddy of them all is **Szimpla Kert** (MAP: 28 P112 C8; *szimpla.hu*), which some say is still the best and most eccentric. **Instant-Fogas** (MAP: 29 P112 D6; *instant-fogas.com*) is where two ruin bars merged to form the biggest in town, with dozens of rooms in which to get lost. Another enormous venue is **Füge Udvar** (MAP: 30 P112 D7; *fugeudvar.hu*), which has a large covered courtyard and lots of side rooms with music and games, while **Kőleves Kert** (MAP: 31 P112 C7; *kolevesvendeglo.hu*) is a chilled and brightly decorated garden club.

LISTINGS

Best Places for...

Ⓔ Budget **ⒺⒺ** Midrange **ⒺⒺⒺ** Top End

Eating

Local Food

Menza ⒺⒺ
32 C5

Retro-chic with a modern take on Hungarian cuisine and some international favourites thrown in. *11am-11pm*

Gettó Gulyás ⒺⒺ
33 C7

The best place to try hearty and meaty *pörkölt* (traditional Hungarian beef stew) and *gulyás* (traditional Hungarian beef soup) in the district. *noon-11pm*

Marumba ⒺⒺ
34 C7

The best dishes of the Carpathian Basin, plus Hungarian natural wines. *5-11pm Mon-Wed, from noon Thu-Sun*

Kőleves ⒺⒺ
35 C7

Always buzzy and lots of fun, Kőleves attracts a young crowd with its Jewish-inspired (but not kosher) menu, lively decor, great service and reasonable prices. *noon-10pm Tue, Wed & Sun, to 11pm Thu-Sat*

Drinking

Night Out

360 Bar
36 C5

This lively rooftop bar mixes all the classic cocktails, but the cherry on top is the out-of-this-world view. *5pm-midnight Mon-Wed, 2pm-2am Thu-Sat, to midnight Sun*

Havana
37 D6

In one of the city's prettiest leafy courtyards, Havana is a Cuban restaurant and bar with live music and dancers most nights. *5pm-midnight Wed & Thu, to 3am Fri & Sat*

Twentysix Budapest
38 B6

A wow location and a wow, plant-filled atrium and tasty cocktails. *7.30am-midnight Sun-Thu, to 2am Fri & Sat*

See p112 for map of locations

Shopping

Vintage Wonders

Gouba-Gozsdu bazár
39 B7

A lovely flea market at Gozsdu Courtyard (p121), where you can pick up interesting pieces from local artists and designers, plus souvenirs. *10am-5pm Fri-Mon*

LoveChild Vintage
40 B5

This is where fur, glitter, animal prints, leather and all things shiny gather. *11am-7pm Mon-Sat*

Szputnyik Shop D-20
41 C8

A bright, open space stuffed with retro fashion. *10am-8pm Mon-Sat, to 6pm Sun*

Retrock
42 A7

Hip store with a vast collection of vintage clothing, bags, jewellery, shoes and Hungarian streetwear. *11am-8pm Mon-Sat, from noon Sun*

See p136 for eating, drinking and shopping listings

Explore
Southern Pest

The colourful districts of Józsefváros (Joseph Town) and Ferencváros (Francis, or Franz, Town) are traditionally working class and full of students. It's fun to wander the backstreets and peep into courtyards. Both are evolving areas, with new venues popping up constantly around hubs such as Mikszáth Kálmán tér and Ráday utca.

From Blaha Lujza tér, the Big Ring Rd runs through Józsefváros. The western side of the district transforms from a neighbourhood of lovely 19th-century townhouses and villas around the Little Ring Rd to a large student quarter. East of the boulevard is a once-rough-and-tumble district now being developed at breakneck speed. South of Üllői út, Ferencváros is home to Budapest's most popular football team, Ferencvárosi Torna Club (FTC), and its green-clad supporters.

Getting Around

 Tram

Józsefváros and Ferencváros are both served by trams 47 and 49, and further east by trams 4 and 6.

 Metro

The M2 metro line runs along the northern border of Józsefváros, while the M3 line serves points in Ferencváros. The M4 line handily connects Fővám tér with Keleti train station. Key stops include Blaha Lujza tér and Keleti pályaudvar on the M2, Corvin-negyed on the M3, Rákóczi tér on the M4 and Kálvin tér where the M3 and M4 intersect.

Café, Mikszáth Kálmán tér
ILPO MUSTO/ALAMY STOCK PHOTO ©

THE BEST

ARCHITECTURE Museum of Applied Arts (p134)

CRAFT BEER Élesztőház (p137)

LIVE MUSIC Jedermann Cafe (p135)

HISTORIC SITE Kerepesi Cemetery (p134)

WINE TASTING Tasting Table (p134)

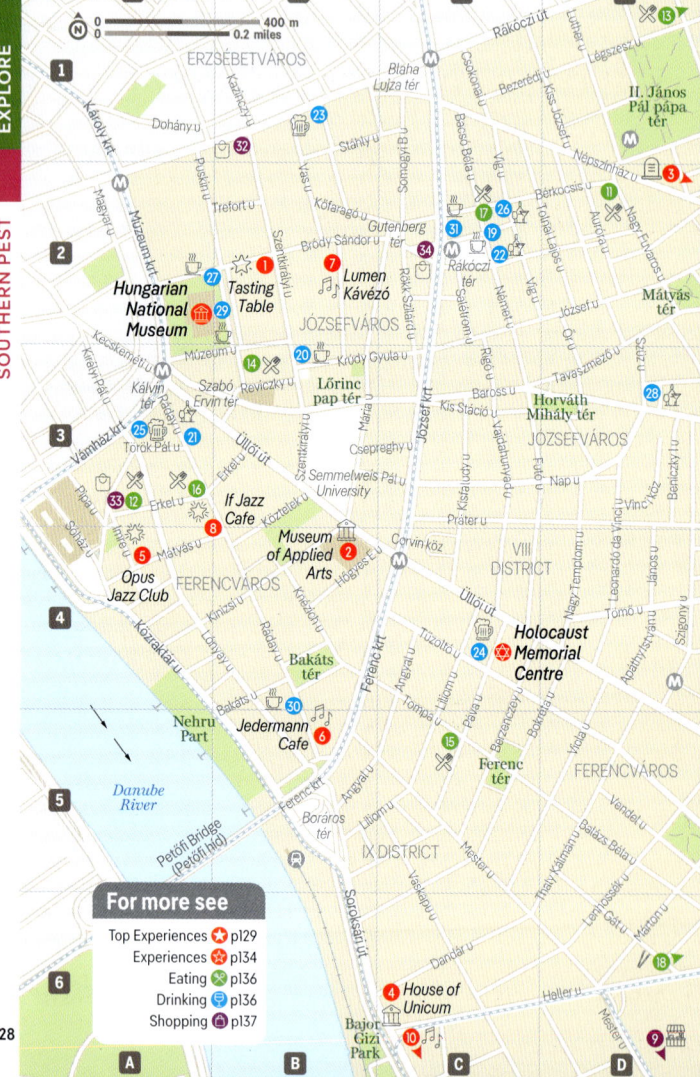

★ TOP EXPERIENCE

Holocaust Memorial Centre

This centre is the only public collection in the country that deals exclusively with the history of the Holocaust. The thematic permanent exhibition traces the rise of anti-Semitism in Hungary and follows the path to the genocide of the country's Jewish and Roma communities.

MAP: **C4**

Death March

Enter the museum via the **Tower of Lost Communities**, remembering the 1400-plus Jewish villages that ceased to exist after WWII. The exhibits in eight rooms consist of a series of maps, photographs, diaries and graphic videos. The personal effects contained in glass columns at the start are moving. The music starts off rather festive, but the displays are accompanied by the sounds of a pounding heartbeat and marching as the doomed are deprived of their freedom and dignity and deported to death camps in Germany and Poland.

Synagogue Reborn

A sublimely restored **synagogue** in the central courtyard, designed by Leopold Baumhorn and completed in 1924, hosts temporary exhibitions on the mezzanine level.

Wall of Remembrance

An 8m-high glass wall in the inner courtyard bears the names of 180,000 Hungarian Holocaust victims and is constantly updated. Labels reading 'anonymous' remind visitors of the many victims whose identities are unknown. A number of plaques and memorials in the garden honour 'righteous gentiles' – the pebbles placed below them signify respect and loss.

PLANNING TIPS
There's an airport-like security check at the centre's entrance, so leave sharp objects back in your room. Visiting the temporary exhibits in the synagogue costs an extra 1500/1000Ft (*adult/concession*).

Scan for opening hours and to book ahead.

★ TOP EXPERIENCE

Hungarian National Museum

This treasure trove of a museum houses the nation's most important collection of historic relics. It traces the history of the Carpathian Basin from the Stone Age and that of the Magyar people and Hungary from the 9th-century conquest to the fall of communism.

MAP: P128 **A2**

PLANNING TIP
A scale model of the museum below the main steps from where the poet Sándor Petőfi recited his 'Nemzeti Dal' (National Song) on 15 March 1848, sparking revolution, will help you with orientation.

Scan this QR code for full opening hours and to book ahead.

Backstory
The museum was founded in 1802 when Count Ferenc Széchényi donated his personal collection of more than 20,000 prints, maps, manuscripts, coins and archaeological finds to the state. It's housed in an impressive Neoclassical edifice purpose-built in 1847 by architect Mihály Pollack.

Coronation Mantle
The room immediately to the left of the grand internal staircase on the 1st floor contains the museum's most precious object: King Stephen's beautiful crimson silk coronation mantle, stitched by nuns in 1031. It was refashioned in the 13th century and the much-faded cloth features an intricate embroidery of fine gold thread and pearls with likenesses of the 12 Apostles, Old Testament prophets and the king-saint himself.

Between East & West
To the right of the same staircase, exhibits in 10 rooms look at the development of the Carpathian Basin from prehistory to the Magyars' arrival in the 9th century.

Birth of Hungary
On the 2nd floor, on either side of the 19th-century Ceremonial Hall (pictured), the history

MITZO/SHUTTERSTOCK ©

lesson continues through 20 rooms – from the Árpád dynasty and the 16th-century Turkish occupation on one side, to the wars of independence, the Habsburg Empire, the two world wars and the rise and fall of communism on the other.

The highlight for many will be the last two rooms, which examine Hungary's role in WWII, the 1956 Uprising and the decades of subsequent communist rule. There's footage from 1956, a mock-up of a secret-police office, *samizdat* (anti-establishment) publications, part of the barbed-wire fence that once separated Hungary from Austria and a town sign from Leninváros (Lenin Town), which reverted to its original name, Tiszaújváros, only in 1991. Best of all, there's the hand of the monster-sized Stalin statue that once graced City Park.

QUICK BREAK
Geraldine (p137), a branch of the celebrated Auguszt pastry chain in the museum's Garden House, is one of Budapest's most beautiful cafes. Enjoy exquisite cakes and coffee in sumptuous surrounds.

Walk from Market to Market

The ideal way to appreciate these two fascinating but large, traditionally working-class districts is to pick a sight and then spend time wandering in the nearby streets. This area, set between excellent markets, is filled with antiquarian bookshops, ghosts from the 1956 Uprising and some unusual architecture.

START	END	LENGTH
Nagycsarnok	Rákóczi tér	1.3km; one to two hours

1. Bountiful Market

Nagycsarnok, Budapest's largest market, attracts tourists in droves, but it's so big that the crowds easily disperse. Downstairs are local food products such as potted foie gras, garlands of dried paprika, souvenir sacks and tins of paprika powder, honey, meat and lavender. Head up to the 1st floor for Hungarian folk costumes, dolls, painted eggs and embroidered tablecloths as well as cooked foods such as *kolbász* (sausage), *pörkölt* (stew) and *lángos* (fried dough).

2. Span Stories

Just opposite, in the northern tollhouse of Liberty Bridge, is a tiny exhibition called **Connected**, a branch of the Hungarian Technical and Transportation Museum that looks at the histories of the half-dozen bridges spanning the Danube in central Budapest.

3. Browsing History

The western side of Múzeum körút is lined with shops selling antiquarian and secondhand books. Our favourite is the **Múzeum Antikvárium**, just opposite the Hungarian National Museum. Further north is **Központi Antikvárium**, the largest and oldest in town.

4. Parliament Sat Here

Follow Bródy Sándor utca east to **Bródy House**. Now a boutique hotel with the superb **Garden Cafe** (p137), this place would have lots of tales to tell could it speak. It was the residence of Hungary's prime minister in the 19th century, when Parliament sat next door at No 8. If you don't believe us, just look at the back of the 20,000Ft note.

5. Palace 'Hood

This neighbourhood is often called Palota-negyed – the Palace Quarter – because of its impressive 19th-century mansions. A favourite is **Gschwindt Palace**, at the end of the block. It was built at the turn of the century by a successful wine producer and merchant, whose bust you can see above the entrance.

6. Call to Arms

On the evening of 23 October 1956, ÁVH government agents fired on a group of protesters gathering outside these **radio headquarters** after they began shouting anti-Soviet slogans and demanding that reformist Imre Nagy be named prime minister. By morning, Budapest was in revolution.

7. Traditional Marketplace

Rákóczi tér has sported a handsome and authentic market hall since 1897. Inside you'll find the usual staples – fruit, veg, cured meats, cheese, jam and baked goods – with some folks bringing their produce in direct from the farm.

EXPERIENCES

Taste Wine with the Experts
WINE TASTING

MAP: ❶ P128 B2

For a crash course in Hungarian wine, head for the cellars of **Tasting Table** *(tastehungary.com)*. Tastings of between five *(17,500Ft)* and eight *(23,000Ft)* wines, paired with a tasty cheese and charcuterie board, are held daily at 3pm and 6pm. Knowledgeable staff will walk you through each wine. At its shop across the road, you can taste and order flights *(5,800Ft)* without prebooking.

Admiring Art Nouveau
ARCHITECTURE

MAP: ❷ P128 B4

Housed in a gorgeous Art Nouveau building (1896) designed by Ödön Lechner and decorated with Zsolnay ceramic tiles, the **Museum of Applied Arts** *(imm.hu)* is undergoing renovations and has been closed since 2017. You might get lucky and chance upon one of the special exhibits occasionally held in the completed Glass Hall, a blindingly white, atrium-like extravaganza said to be modelled on Spain's Alhambra.

Digging up the Past
CEMETERY

MAP: ❸ P128 D2

Kerepesi Cemetery *(fiumeiutisir kert.nori.gov.hu)* is Budapest's version of London's Highgate or Paris' Père Lachaise. Some of the 3000-plus graves and mausoleums in the 56-hectare necropolis are worthy of a pharaoh, especially those of political leaders and national heroes such as Lajos Kossuth, Ferenc Deák and Lajos Batthyány. Plot 21 contains the graves of many who died in the 1956 Uprising. Sitting uncomfortably close by is the huge Workers' Movement Pantheon for party honchos topped with the words, 'I lived for Communism, for the people'. Just north is the simple grave of János Kádár (1912–89), whose tomb was desecrated in 2007. The cemetery is open 7am to 8pm May to July, to 5pm March, to 7pm April and August, to 6pm September and 7.30am to 5pm October to February.

 SHAKE, RATTLE & ROLL

Hungarians can be masters of the macabre. Who else could have produced the likes of Béla Lugosi? But that's hardly as ghoulish as things get here. János Kádár, the not-much-missed former communist leader, had been resting in plot 12 for almost 18 years at Kerepesi Cemetery when, in May 2007, a person or persons unknown crept into the graveyard, broke into his coffin and ran off with comrade Kádár's skull and assorted bones, leaving behind a note that read: 'Murderers and traitors may not rest in holy ground 1956–2006'. The remains have still not been found.

Sup Something Unique   DISTILLERY
MAP: ④ P128 C6

Unicum, the thick, almost-medicinal-tasting aperitif made from 40 herbs and spices and dating back to 1790, is as bitter as a loser's tears and a favourite drink in Hungary. Explore its history at the **House of Unicum** (*unicumhaz.hu; adult/under 18 4700/3300Ft*) and its museum. The 90-minute guided tour starts with a video, demonstrates the distilling process in the cellar and ends with a tasting session of two/four types of Unicum.

Searching for Diamonds in the Rough   FLEA MARKET
MAP: ⑨ P128 D6

Some consider a visit to **Ecseri Piac** (*piaconline.hu*) as the consummate Budapest experience. One of the biggest flea markets in Central Europe, Ecseri sells everything from antique jewellery and Soviet army watches to top hats. Early Saturday is the best time to go. The flea market is about 10km southeast of the Nagycsarnok. To get there, take bus 54 from Pest's Boráros tér or, for a quicker journey, express bus 84E, 89E or 94E from the Határ út stop on the M3 metro line.

Hearing Near-perfect Classical Music   CONCERT HALL
MAP: ⑩ P128 C6

They may not have the romantic surrounds of the Hungarian State Opera House or the Liszt Music Academy, but the two concert venues in the **Palace of Art** (*mupa.hu*) in the Millenniuminegyed (Millennium Quarter) on the Danube embankment make up for that with near-perfect acoustics. Catch a full orchestral performance at the 1700-seat Béla Bartók National Concert Hall, or a string quartet at the more intimate Festival Theatre, which seats 450 people.

BEST SPOTS FOR LIVE JAZZ

Opus Jazz Club
MAP: ⑤ P128 A4

Hungarian and international jazz groups take to the stage at the Budapest Music Center five times a week from Tuesday to Saturday at 8pm. *opusjazzclub.hu*

Jedermann Cafe
MAP: ⑥ P128 B5

This intimate, old-style cafe-restaurant turns into a great music venue on Friday and Saturday at 9pm, focusing primarily on jazz. *jedermann.hu*

Lumen Kávézó
MAP: ⑦ P128 B2

This large venue with multiple rooms and covered and open courtyards has music most nights. *facebook.com/lumen.kavezo*

If Jazz Cafe
MAP: ⑧ P128 A3

Small but perfectly formed, this cafe-restaurant has nightly concerts at 8pm. *if-jazz-cafe-budapest.hu*

LISTINGS

Best Places for...

B Budget **BB** Midrange **BBB** Top End

See p128 for map of locations

Eating

Hungarian

Öcsi B
 D2

For the closest thing to homemade Hungarian food, head to this very authentic *étkezde* (diner) for weekday lunch. *11.30am-2.30pm Mon-Fri*

Borbíróság BB
12 A3

Relaxed yet classy 'Wine Court' offering Hungarian wines by the glass. Takes its food – especially duck – pretty seriously. *noon-11.30pm Mon-Sat*

Rosenstein BBB
13 D1

A chic, family-run Hungarian restaurant in an unlikely location, with Jewish tastes and super service. Interesting game dishes. *noon-11pm Mon-Sat*

Other European

Arquitecto Pitpit BB
14 B3

An authentic slice of Spain in a lovely hidden courtyard with a great range of tapas. *5-11pm Mon-Sat*

Paletta Bistró BB
15 C5

This neighbourhood eatery offers international dishes (shakshuka, Argentine stuffed pizza), but its signature is *rántott sajt* (breaded and deep-fried cheese). *11.30am-10.30pm Mon-Sat, 10am-4pm Sun*

Tefliso BB
 A3

Georgian cuisine has always had a large fanbase in Budapest and this popular place serves seven types of *khachapuri* (cheese-stuffed bread). *noon-11pm*

African & Asian

African Buffet B
17 C2

We love the homemade food, the colourful decor and the warm welcome at this little family-run African oasis near the Rákóczi tér market. *11am-10pm Mon-Fri*

Hanoi Xua BB
 D6

This place, opposite the Natural History Museum, has an authentic menu of pho, *bún* (rice noodles) and other Vietnamese favourites. *11am-8.30pm Mon-Thu, to 9.30pm Fri-Sun*

Drinking

Pubs & Bars

Café Csiga
19 C2

The 'Snail Cafe' is a very popular, welcoming place facing the Rákóczi tér market, with relaxed space on two levels that attracts a hipster crowd. *9am-midnight*

Tilos a Tilos
20 B3

The anchor tenant in a car-free square, this cafe/bar's huge terrace is always overflowing with students. *9am-midnight Mon-Fri, from noon Sat & Sun*

Púder Bárszínház
 A3

This erstwhile theatre filled with stuffed animals and dolls' heads is a popular bar with food and a dynamic cultural space. *noon-midnight Sun & Tue,*

to 1am Wed & Thu, to 2am Fri & Sat

Oinos
 C2

Housed in the Rákóczi tér market building, this is a fully fledged bistro serving brunch and Mediterranean dishes as well a sophisticated wine bar. *8am-11pm*

Craft Beer

Stifler Beerhouse & Kitchen
23 **B1**

Spacious temple to microbrewed ale and lager with some 20 brews on tap, including two from local Horizont Brewing. *noon-midnight Sun-Thu, to 1am Fri & Sat*

Élesztőház
24 **C4**

A ruin pub set in a former glassblowing workshop offering an unrivalled selection of 30 craft beers on tap. *3pm-3am*

Monyo Tap House
25 **A3**

Long-established pub on central Kálvin tér 7 with 10 craft beers on tap (one always local) and another 30 in bottles. *noon-midnight Mon-Thu, to 1am Fri, 5pm-midnight Sat*

Macska
 C2

The cosy and funky 'Cat' is a peculiar little cafe-bar, with excellent craft beer and decent veggie and vegan dishes. *4pm-midnight Mon-Thu, to 2am Fri*

Cafes

Garden Cafe
27 **A2**

This antiques-cluttered cafe with garden seating at Brody House is perfect for brunch or just a speciality coffee at any time. *8am-4pm*

Nem Adom Fel Kávézó és Étterem
28 **D3**

'I Won't Give Up' is Hungary's first cafe and restaurant (try the goodies-filled vegan box) operated by people with special needs and disabilities. *9am-4pm Mon-Fri*

Geraldine
29 **B2**

Cafe occupying an outbuilding at the national museum, serving exquisite cakes and pastries in regal surrounds. *10am-7pm Tue-Sun*

Nándor Cukrászda
30 **B4**

This tiny patisserie with excellent biscuits and cakes has been here since 1957 and there's always a queue. *7.30am-7pm Mon-Sat*

Vaj
 C2

'Butter' serves sandwiches, pastries and other light fare in airy, industrial digs on the edge of Rákóczi tér. Speciality coffees and cocktails, too. *7am-8pm*

Shopping

Food & Drink

Magyar Pálinka Háza
32 **B1**

This large shop stocks hundreds of varieties of *pálinka* (fruit brandy) as well as *pálinka*-filled chocolates. *9am-7pm Mon-Fri, to 4pm Sat*

Taste the World
33 **A3**

Enormous supermarket with the widest selection of spices, seasonings and Asian foodstuffs you'll find anywhere. *10am-6pm Mon, 9am-6.30pm Tue-Fri, to 3pm Sat*

Music & Books

Liszt Ferenc Zeneműbolt
34 **C2**

The Ferenc Liszt Music Shop, stocked with mostly classical CDs as well as sheet music and books of local interest, shares space with a branch of the Libra Books chain. *10am-6pm Mon-Fri, to 2pm Sat*

★ WORTH A TRIP

City Park

Serene City Park (Városliget) is a heavyweight when it comes to sights. It's home to mega museums, Budapest's most impressive square, a zoo, Széchenyi Baths and even a castle. Away from the attractions are towering trees, a lovely lake and playgrounds.

MAP: P140

PLANNING TIP
Zooming around the park is speedy and fun on a bike or electric scooter. It's easy to rent either – look for the green MOL Bubi bike-sharing stations, or pick up an electric Lime scooter through the app.

Scan this QR code for news and updates.

An Elegant Entrance

Forming a stunning gateway to the park, **Heroes' Square** is Budapest's largest and most emblematic square. Its centrepiece is the Millennium Monument, erected in 1896 to mark the 1000th anniversary of the Magyar conquest of the Carpathian Basin in the late 9th century. Two colonnades display 14 key Hungarian leaders, while, in the middle, a towering obelisk is topped by a statue of Archangel Gabriel – legend has it that Pope Sylvester II dreamed that the angel offered St Stephen the crown of Hungary. At the column's base are the seven chieftains who led the Magyars into the Carpathian Basin, while the Tomb of the Unknown Soldier commemorates those who died defending the country throughout history. It's particularly majestic at night.

Museum of Fine Arts

Housed in a grand Neoclassical building, the **Museum of Fine Arts** *(szepmuveszeti.hu; adult/student 5800/2900Ft)* is home to an impressive collection of foreign and local works dating from antiquity to the present day. The ground floor's Romanesque, Renaissance and Baroque halls are sights to behold.

Vajdahunyad Castle

The architectural eye candy that is **Vajdahunyad Castle** (pictured right) was built originally from wood and later from stone in 1896 for Hungary's millenary celebrations, aiming to showcase the

KURKA GEZA COREY/SHUTTERSTOCK ©

country's different architectural styles over the previous 1000 years. It's currently home to the **Hungarian Agricultural Museum** *(mezogazdasagimuzeum.hu; adult/student 3000/1500Ft)*, displaying all things agricultural. Don't miss the Hall of Hunting, where hundreds of antlers fill rooms with Gothic arched ceilings – a hauntingly cool sight. Its two towers, the Apostles' Tower and the Gatehouse Tower, can be climbed for views.

Széchenyi Baths

All-round splendid **Széchenyi Baths** *(szechenyifurdo.hu; 8400-14000Ft)* are Europe's largest medicinal baths. While the indoor section feels like a fun labyrinth, the exterior is stunning, with sunflower-yellow Neoclassical design contrasting vividly with the blue waters. Special amenities such as a beer bath, Saturday 'sparties' (spa+party, right?) and a Palm House also feature.

QUICK BREAK

The epitome of Hungarian gastronomy, **Gundel** *(gundel.hu)* is one of the most famous restaurants in Hungary. Choose from the 'National 11' menu to sample iconic Hungarian dishes.

TRY A SIP OF HEALING WATER

Healing thermal waters from Széchenyi Baths (p139) are sold at a super-cheap price in a separate building behind the baths.

Budapest Zoo

The enormous **Budapest Zoo** *(zoobudapest.com; adult/child 5000/3500Ft)* is home to nearly 1000 different species of animals. It's also an architectural wonder, with an Art Nouveau entrance and Elephant House and a Palm House designed by Gustave Eiffel (of Eiffel Tower fame).

BalloonFly

A huge **hot-air balloon** *(balloonfly.hu; adult/child 8500/5000Ft)* northeast of Vajdahunyad Castle takes passengers for a 150m flight above City Park.

Városliget Lake

Just behind Heroes' Sq, **Városliget Lake** is beloved by locals. From spring to autumn, you can rent colourful pedalos and SUPs to float around and enjoy the views to Vajdahunyad Castle. In winter, the lake turns into Europe's largest outdoor ice-skating rink.

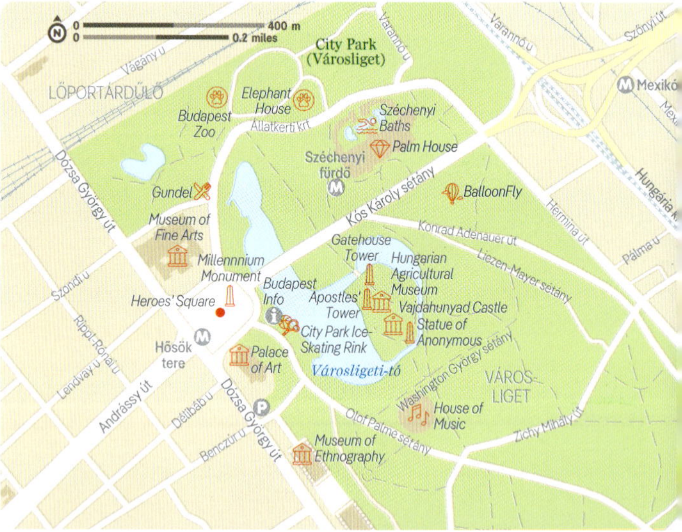

Statue of Anonymous

Opposite Vajdahunyad Castle, the **statue** of a mysterious hooded figure is Anonymous, the unknown chronicler credited with writing the earliest book on Hungarian history, Gesta Hungarorum. According to local lore, Anonymous bestows inspiration on all writers who touch the quill in his hand.

House of Music

Nestled among the park's trees, the **House of Music** (zenehaza.hu) is an architecturally astonishing building designed by famed Japanese architect, Sou Fujimoto. It's a concert venue, museum and education centre in one. The permanent exhibition is outstanding, exploring centuries of European and Hungarian music, from the mysticism of shamanic drumming to modern movie soundtracks. Outside, a unique playground invites visitors to make music with their movements.

Palace of Art

Facing the Museum of Fine Arts across Heroes' Sq, the beautiful building reminiscent of a Greek temple is the **Palace of Art** (mucsarnok.hu; adult/student 4900/2500Ft), the best place to view contemporary art in the city. It stages four to five major temporary exhibitions throughout the year, promoting Hungarian and international visual arts, as well as occasional concerts.

Museum of Ethnography

Opened in 2022, the **Museum of Ethnography's** (neprajz.hu) main attraction is the walkable parabolic rooftop garden, providing views from its highest points. Inside, the collection displays some 3600 original, restored artefacts from Hungary all the way to Africa.

Between its wings, a triangular monument commemorates the 50th anniversary of Hungary's 1956 Uprising at the very spot from where a huge statue of Stalin was pulled down by demonstrators and sawed apart until only its boots remained – a replica of the boots is on display at Memento Park (p62).

STOLEN ART

When you're inside the Museum of Fine Arts (p138), note that one of its most famous paintings, Raphael's *Esterházy Madonna*, was once broken in half, thanks to the greatest art theft in Hungary's history in 1983. The theft was a Hungarian-Italian job.

Budapest Toolkit

Family Travel 144

Accommodation 145

Food, Drink & Nightlife 146

LGBTIQ+ Travellers 148

Health & Safe Travel 149

Responsible Travel 150

Accessible Travel 152

Nuts & Bolts 153

Language 154

Funicular (p43), Castle District
IGOR DYMOV/SHUTTERSTOCK ©

Family Travel

Hungary is extremely family-friendly, with loads of attractions for the young, old and everyone in between. There's plenty to keep the little ones occupied, from zoos to outstanding playgrounds and kid-oriented museums.

Family-friendly Spas

Though children under 14 are not allowed to use the thermal pools at historic baths – some such as Rudas or Veli Bej won't even let them enter – the outdoor sections are different. Family-friendly water parks include **Palatinus Strand** (p103) and **Aquaworld** (p103).

PLAYTIME

City Park (p138) is home to one of the capital's coolest playgrounds, Main Playground, occupying more than 13,000 sq metres and housing a three-storey hot-air-balloon-shaped climbing frame.

Scan the QR code for more details.

Santa Claus is Coming to Town

In Hungary, Santa Claus *(Mikulás)* comes to town early, on 6 December, the feast day of St Nicholas, with his two helpers: a good angel and the mean, hairy and horned creature called krampusz. At this time of year, family-friendly events take place across the city, and the real Finnish Joulupukki (Christmas goat) often visits the **Vörösmarty tér Christmas Fair**.

Getting Around

Children under six travel for free on Budapest's public transport. Older kids with an EU student card get a discount.

Family Tickets

Almost all museums and attractions offer discounted family tickets, or free or reduced admission for the little ones.

Dining Out

Most restaurants have a kids' menu *(gyerekmenü)* that includes crowd-pleasers such as chicken nuggets, fries and spaghetti. If not, you can ask for a half-portion serving, or a simple dish made especially for them.

Accommodation

From flawless luxury to a dormitory bed and everything in between, Budapest has accommodation options galore for all budgets.

Where to Stay if you Love...

History, Views & Quiet
Not necessarily the cheapest, but the **Castle District** (p33) is home to major historic sights, great museums, cute cobblestone streets and the loveliest views.

Bar Hopping, Street Art & Lively Nights
Inner **Erzsébetváros** (p111) is Budapest's unofficial party quarter with cool nightlife spots and crowds. Outer Erzsébetváros is close to the happening part of town, but without the noise.

Hikes, Nature & Greenery
Óbuda and the Buda Hills (p65) offer a few lovely guesthouses close to hiking trails, caves and greenery. Óbuda feels like an old-timey village, just 20 minutes from the city centre.

Shopping, Cafes & Restaurants
Belváros (p77), or the Inner Town, is the centre of Pest's universe, close to pretty much everything, and full of cafes, shops and restaurants.

Sightseeing & Galleries
The **Parliament** (p87) area is home to iconic sights, great galleries, excellent restaurants and welcoming cafes and bars. And **Margaret Island** (p101) is close by.

HOW MUCH FOR A NIGHT IN A

Hostel dorm bed: from **3000Ft**

Midrange hotel: from **25,000Ft**

Five-star hotel: from **60,000Ft**

OUR PICK
We Love to Stay in...

City Park (p138). This park is Pest's green lung, with picnic spots, jogging trails and a lovely lake, but it's also home to a handful of heavyweight sights and family-friendly attractions. The area around the park includes hotels and apartments on calm streets, while the city centre is a comfortable 15 minutes away.

Food, Drink & Nightlife

Allergies & Intolerances

Allergens such as nuts, dairy and gluten are almost always openly listed on restaurant menus in Budapest, but it's always best to communicate your intolerances to your waiter.

HOW TO SAY

I'm allergic to...	**Allergiás vagyok...** *(ahl-lehr-gyahsh-vah- dyawk)*
gluten	**glutén** *(glu-ten)*
dairy products	**tejtermék** *(they-tehr-meek)*
nuts	**magok** *(magh-ohk)*
seafood	**tengeri ételek** *(ten-geh-ree eh-teh-lek)*

HOW TO ASK...

Is this gluten free?
Ez gluténmentes? *(ehz-glue-ten-men-tesh)*

Does this contain nuts?
Vannak benne magvak? *(van-nahk-ben-neh-magg-vack)*

Is there a vegan option?
Van vegan opció? *(vahn-ve-ghan-op-tsee-yo)*

TRY PÁLINKA

Pálinka (fruit brandy) is the country's most revered beverage. Traditionally, *pálinka* should be served at room temperature in a tulip-shaped glass – round at the bottom, narrow at the rim. Full glasses should be clinked, sipped and savoured, though locals will likely challenge you to gulp it in one go.

Hungarian Food

Traditional Hungarian food is generally rich, hearty and meaty, and paprika and sour cream are superstar ingredients that go into nearly every recipe. Nowadays, vegan and vegetarian dishes are more widely available. *Pörkölt* (meat or mushroom stew), *lángos* (deep-fried disk-shaped dough) and *kürtőskalács* (a sweet dough 'chimney cake') are must-trys.

HOW TO... Pay the Bill

Asking for the bill: When you're ready to pay, say '*A számlát legyenszíves*' (The bill, please). Pronounced o saam-laat- le-dyen-see-vesh.

Splitting the bill: Generally, the bill comes in one sum. To make sure, the waiter might ask '*Egybe vagy külön?*' (Together or separate?). Pronounced ehj-beh vaj kew-lawn?

Paying: You can pay by cash *(készpénz)* or card *(kártya)*. Pronounced kays-paynz (cash) and kar-tyah (card). Say '*Készpénzzel vagy kártyával fizetnék*' (I would like to pay by cash or card). Pronounced kays-paynz-ehl vadj kar-tyah-val fiz-et-nayk.

Tipping: A service charge *(szervízdíj)* of about 12% might already be included in the bill, in which case further tipping isn't required.

PRICE RANGES

The following price ranges refer to the average cost of a main course.
€ less than 10,000Ft
€€ 10,000-15,000Ft
€€€ more than 15,000Ft

OPENING HOURS

Cafes 8am to 8pm
Restaurants 10am to 10pm
Bakeries 6am to 6pm

Going Out

Erzsébetváros Inner District VII is Budapest's de facto party quarter, with an endless number of pubs and bars. Ruin bars, unique to Budapest, are a dime a dozen here, but the standout one is **Szimpla Kert** (p124). **Gozsdu Courtyard** (p121) is a long passageway with bars and clubs on both sides and always buzzing with life.

Bartók Béla út Not far from Gellért Hill in District XI, Bartók Béla út is the happening part of Buda. It's full of cool cafes, pubs and bars, but is much quieter and more local than Erzsébetváros.

Beer bars Budapest has a solid selection of local brews that are worth a try. Head to **Élesztőház** (p137) for a start.

Concerts Summer-only Budapest Park is one of the city's main concert venues, boasting festival-like vibes, while **A38** (p60), housed on a decommissioned Ukrainian cargo ship and offering something for pretty much every night, is one of the coolest.

HOW MUCH FOR A

Cup of coffee
500-1500Ft

Cafe breakfast
1500-3000Ft

Pint of beer
600-2200Ft

Kürtőskalács (chimney cake)
800-1500Ft

Lángos (fried dough)
1000-2000Ft

Glass of wine
800-1800Ft

Meal at a restaurant
3000-8000Ft

LGBTIQ+ Travellers

While Budapest has a solid gay scene, the country's stance on LGBTIQ+ issues is out of step with many other parts of Europe.

An Outdated Mindset

Compared with Western European countries, Hungary's LGBTIQ+ scene has a long way to go. The government strongly promotes a conservative Christian agenda and still enacts anti-LGBTIQ+ laws, while negative attitudes in older generations linger. Though travellers aren't affected, most gay people are discreet in public places and PDAs are rare.

Younger generations are generally open, friendly and accepting, and Budapest has a lively and diverse gay scene with bars, events and parties where visitors also have a good time. Though the city doesn't have a 'rainbow district' like other European capitals, bars welcome all, and some are specifically gay-friendly and host events such as drag shows or drag-night bingo.

OUR PICKS

By Day of the Week

MONDAY Gólya Presszó Visit this young and free-spirited community centre.
TUESDAY Gaby's Try to catch a themed event like Taco Tuesday.
WEDNESDAY Why Not Gay-friendly riverside bar.
THURSDAY Tuk Tuk Bar Cocktails inside the Casati Budapest Hotel.
FRIDAY CoXx Check out 'Horny Friday' at the city's only gay-cruise club.
SATURDAY Alterego Party at the city's premier gay club.
SUNDAY Habroló Enjoy live piano music.

BUDAPEST PRIDE

June's Budapest Pride is Hungary's largest annual LGBTIQ+ event. The main happening is a colourful parade, leading to a rave Rainbow Party in Budapest Park.

LET LOOSE

K!NK is a regular underground LGBTIQ+ techno event with wild outfits and no photos. Scan the QR code for upcoming events.

Resources

- **Family Is Family** A civil initiative spreading awareness about the situation of rainbow families: *acsaladazcsalad.hu* • **Háttér Society** LGBTIQ+ updates and counselling hotline: *en.hatter.hu* • **Labrisz** Info on the city's lesbian scene: *labrisz.hu*

Health & Safe Travel

Budapest is a super-safe city, but it's still wise to make sensible pre-departure preparations.

WATER

Budapest has plentiful clean water, and tap water is safe to drink and of high quality, according to EU standards. If you're up for tasting mineral-rich thermal water, the healing powers of which locals swear by, head to the drinking halls of **Széchenyi**, **Rudas** or **Lukács** baths.

Drugs

Hungary has some of the harshest drug laws in the EU, and all drugs are of the same 'class', meaning the rules that apply for heroin also apply for cannabis. Purchasing, consuming and possessing illegal drugs are all criminal offences, and foreigners are held accountable to the same rules as locals. Avoid people trying to sell questionable substances in Budapest's party district (inner Erzsébetváros).

Transport

Eating and drinking aren't allowed on public transport, except in special circumstances like during illness or heatwaves.

Smoking

Hungary has strict laws about smoking and vaping. Both are prohibited in public indoor areas, public-transport stations and around playgrounds. Tobacco-related products have been banned from regular shops and supermarkets and can only be bought at national tobacco shops called Nemzeti Dohánybolt. Elf Bar disposable vapes are illegal.

QUICK INFO

Security
Petty crime isn't common in Budapest, but be generally mindful.

Privacy
Photographing people on the street without their permission is technically illegal.

Thermal Baths
Bathing in thermal water isn't recommended for pregnant women and children under 14.

SCAMS

Avoid people aggressively selling stuff on the street. If a transport ticket machine isn't giving back coins, check if the coin slot has tape over it.

Responsible Travel

Follow these tips to leave a lighter footprint, support local businesses and have a positive impact on communities.

Recycle

When you buy a plastic bottle or cans, you'll pay a deposit of 50Ft – look for '50Ft' surrounded by arrows on the label. Once it's empty, you can return the bottle or can to machines found at all bigger shops in Budapest. You'll receive a voucher that you can use in store, deducting the deposit from the final amount of your purchase, or convert to cash.

Go Paperless
Download the **BudapestGO** app *(go.bkk.hu),* where you can buy and store all your tickets and passes for the city's public transport system, ditching paper.

On Feet or Wheels
Budapest is a very walkable city and you can get to all major sights using public transport. If you're up for exploring the city on two wheels, there are many bike-rental places, or you can use the city's official bike-sharing scheme, the green **MOL Bubi** bikes. There are plenty of stations around town where you can pick up and leave bikes.

OUR PICK

Premier Kultcafé
A lovely place that gives back to the community is **Premier KultCafé** *(premiercafe.hu),* a cafe, bakery and cinema in one that employs people with disabilities.

Resources
- **bikemaffia.com** Philanthropic organisation on wheels.
- **worldpackers.com** International website for volunteering opportunities.
- **budapestinfo.hu** Up-to-date and useful information on everything Budapest.

SHOP LOCAL

Budapest has lovely market halls such as **Nagycsarnok** (p133) and the **Rákóczi tér Market Hall** (p133), full of fresh produce and local delicacies. On Sundays, a farmers market sets up at **Szimpla Kert** (p124).

Secondhand Shopping

Budapest is a real treasure trove of preloved stuff. **Ecseri Piac** (p135), on the city's outskirts, is one of the best places to dig for treasure, with everything from furniture to art, old coins, jewellery and even communist memorabilia.

On weekends, a small market sets up shop inside **Gozsdu Courtyard** (p121), selling jewellery, posters, bags and all sorts of knick-knacks.

DRINKING FOUNTAINS

Ditch single-use plastics and find a drinking fountain in Budapest to refill your bottle with clean and fresh drinking water. **Find your nearest fountain using this QR code.**

Climate Change & Travel

It's impossible to ignore the impact we have when travelling; Lonely Planet urges all travellers to engage with their travel carbon footprint, which will mainly come from air travel. While there often isn't an alternative, travellers can look to minimise the number of flights they take, opt for newer aircrafts and use cleaner ground transport, such as trains. One proposed solution–purchasing carbon offsets–unfortunately does not cancel out the impact of individual flights. While most destinations will depend on air travel for the foreseeable future, for now, pursuing ground-based travel where possible is the best course of action.

The **UN carbon footprint calculator** shows how flying impacts a household's emissions.

The **ICAO's Carbon Emissions Calculator** allows visitors to analyse the CO2 generated by point-to-point journeys.

FROM TOP: NICK PASCHALIS/SHUTTERSTOCK ©, RAYPHOTOGRAPHER/SHUTTERSTOCK ©

Accessible Travel

Public Transport
Budapest's public transport system is mostly accessible. The main bus and tram routes in the city centre have low-floor vehicles – some buses are equipped with ramps. M3 and M4 are fully accessible, M2 is partially and M1 isn't accessible. See the BudapestGO app for more details.

Accessible Sightseeing
Most major sights in Budapest are fully accessible. Cobblestone streets in the Castle District might be problematic, but Fisherman's Bastion, Matthias Church and the Hungarian National Gallery are accessible.

FREE TRAVEL
Public transport in Budapest is free for everyone over the age of 65, so long as they have a valid ID card or passport as proof.

Taking a Splash
Out of Budapest's beautiful historic baths, **Gellért** (p52), **Rudas** (p58), **Lukács** (p73) and **Széchenyi** (p139) are accessible. There are accessible bathrooms and changing rooms, and some pools have pool lifts.

OUR PICK
Close to the accessible Arany János M3 station and central Deák tér, the **Basilica of St Stephen** (p92) has an accessible entrance for those with limited mobility, and a calm and contemplative atmosphere ideal for people with sensory sensitivities or those who prefer quieter, less crowded spaces. Its aisles are wide, making it easy for wheelchair users to move around, and the dome's 360-degree view can be reached by a lift. There are many accessible restaurants and cafes close by.

ACCOMMODATION

Budget hotels aren't always accessible, but newer and larger ones usually are. Though many Budapest apartment buildings have lifts and ramps, some Airbnbs might not be accessible – it's best to ask in advance.

Resources
- **Hungarian Federation of Disabled Persons' Associations** *(meosz.hu)*
Travellers with disabilities seeking information can contact this umbrella group.

Nuts & Bolts

Opening Hours

Expect seasonal changes and different hours by location (city centre or outskirts). Normal business hours are 8am to 5pm. Businesses and government offices often close early on Friday afternoon.

Banks 8am-4pm Monday-Friday; some close early on Friday

Bars 4pm-late

Museums 10am-6pm; many close on Monday

Restaurants 10am-10pm; breakfast places open earlier

Shopping centres 10am-9pm

Supermarkets 7am-7, 8 or 9pm; some close early on Saturday and stay closed on Sunday

QUICK INFO

Time zone Central European Time (GMT/UTC +1)

City calling code +36

Emergency number 112

Population 1.7 million

ELECTRICITY

230V/50Hz

230V/50Hz

Toilets

Public toilets in Budapest are rare and often unclean. In restaurants, cafes and bars, only paying guests can use the toilets.

Public Holidays

Shops, banks and public and private offices are closed on Hungary's **National Holidays** *(Nemzeti Ünnep)*. If a holiday falls on a Tuesday or Thursday, the Monday or Friday in between becomes a holiday, and the preceding or following Saturday becomes a business day.

New Year's Day 1 January

Memorial Day of the 1848 Revolution 15 March

Easter March/April

Labour Day 1 May

Whit Monday May/June

Foundation of the State 20 August

Memorial Day of the 1956 Revolution 23 October

All Saints' Day 1 November

Christmas 25-26 December

Nyitva Open

Zárva Closed

Language

Basics

Hello.
Szervusz. *ser·vus*

Goodbye.
Viszont-látásra. *vi·sawnt laa·taash·ro*

Yes.
Igen. *i·gen*

No.
Nem. *nem*

Please.
Kérem. *kay·rem*

Thank you.
Köszönöm. *keu·seu·neum*

You're welcome.
Szívesen. *see·ve·shen*

Excuse me.
Elnézést kérek. *el·nay·zaysht kay·rek*

Fast Phrases

Do you speak English?
Beszél angolul? *be·sayl on·gaw·lul*

I (don't) understand.
(Nem) Értem. *(nem) ayr·tem*

I'd like a/an... **Szeretnék egy...** *se·ret·nayk ej...*
beer. **sör** *sheur*
(cup of) coffee. **(csésze) kávé** *(chay·se) kaa·vay*
glass of wine. **pohár bor** *paw·haar bawr*

Please bring the bill.
Kérem, hozza a számlát. *kay·rem hawz·zo o saam·laat*

How much is this?
Mennyibe kerül ez? *men'·yi·be ke·rewl ez*

Where are the toilets?
Hol a véce? *hawl o vay·tse*

Could you please speak more slowly?
Tudna lassabban beszélni, kérem? *tud·no losh·shob·bon be·sayl·ni, kay·rem*

Where's an ATM?
Hol van egy bankautomata? *hawl von ej bonk·o·u·taw·mo·to*

Could I have a receipt, please?
Kaphatnék egy nyugtát, kérem? *kop·hot·nayk ej nyug·taat kay·rem*

Numbers

 egy *ej*

 kettő *ket·tēū*

 három *haa·rawm*

 négy *nayj*

 öt *eut*

Good to Know

The Hungarian language may look daunting with its long words and unusual-looking accents, but it is surprisingly easy to pronounce.

When two female friends or a man and a woman meet, they may give each other a kiss on both cheeks. Relatives also frequently kiss upon meeting one another. Men, however, normally shake hands. If your hosts or friends go to kiss you, remember to present your left cheek first. A polite greeting from children to adults, or men to women, is: **I kiss your hand** – *Kezét csókolom*. While this is common to hear, you're not actually expected to kiss the person's hand as you say this.

EMERGENCIES

Help! Segítség!
she·geet·shayg

Call the police! Hívja a rendőrséget!
heev·yo o rend·ēūr·shay·get

Call a doctor! Hívjon orvost!
heev·yawn awr·vawsht

I'm lost. Eltévedtem.
el·tay·ved·tem

I'm sick. Rosszul vagyok. *raws·sul vo·dyawk*

Signs

Bejárat Entrance
Kijárat Exit
Férfiak Men
Nők Women
Nyitva Open
Zárva Closed
Információ Information
Mosdó Toilets
Repülőtér Airport
Tilos a dohányzás No smoking

Listen for

Adja ide az útlevelét. *od·yo i·de oz ūt·le·ve·layt*
Your passport, please.
Törölve *teu·reul·ve*
Cancelled.

GREETINGS

On first introduction, Hungarians usually shake hands and say their full names. The family name is said first followed by the first name. As you become more familiar with people, they may suggest you call them by their first name.

 6 **hat** *hot*

 7 **hét** *hayt*

 8 **nyolc** *nyawlts*

 9 **kilenc** *ki·lents*

 10 **tíz** *teez*

Index

Sights 000   Map pages 000

See also separate subindexes for:
- **Eating** p158
- **Drinking** p159
- **Shopping** p159

A

A38 9, 17, 60
accessible travel 152
accommodation 23, 145
activities 22-3, *see also* cycling, hiking, ice-skating, swimming
air travel 24, 27
Andrássy út 122
antique shopping 96-7, 133, *see also* Shopping *subindex*
Aquincum 18, 68
architecture 23, 28-9, 96, 121
arriving 24
art galleries 8, *see also* individual museums

B

Basilica of St Stephen 10, 13, 17, 19, 92-3, 152
bathrooms 153
baths, *see* thermal baths
beer 137
Belváros 77-85, **78-9**
 drinking 84-5
 experiences 82-3
 food 84
 itineraries 80-1, **80**
 shopping 85
 transport 77
 walking tours 80-1, **80**
bicycle travel, *see* cycling
boat travel 12, 16, 21, 82
bridges 16, 42, 59
Buda Hills, *see* Óbuda & the Buda Hills
Budapest Retro Museum 97
Budapest Zoo 15, 17, 19, 140
budget travel 15, 23
bus travel 24-6
business hours 147, 153

C

calling code 153
Castle District 33-47, **34-5**
 drinking 47
 experiences 42-5
 food 46-7
 itineraries 40-1, **40**
 shopping 47
 top experiences 36-9
 transport 33
 walking tours 40-1, **40**
Castle Garden Bazaar 58
Castle Museum 8, 16, 19, 37-9
caves 44, 72
Children's Railway 15, 18, 69
Christmas markets 13, 22-3
churches 19
 Basilica of St Stephen 10, 13, 17, 19, 92-3, 152
 Cave Church 54-5, 57
 Church of St Anne 45
 Margaret Island 106
 Matthias Church 42
City Park 12, 138-41, **140**
climate 22-3
costs 21, 27, 146-7
Csányi5 123
Csontváry, Tivadar Kosztka 39
cycling 26, 82, 150

D

dangers, *see* safe travel
disabilities, travellers with 152
drinking & nightlife 146-7, *see also* Drinking *subindex*
drugs 149

E

Ecseri Piac 14, 135
electricity 153
Elizabeth Lookout Tower 18, 72-3
emergency number 153
Erzsébetváros & the Jewish Quarter 111-25, **112-13**
 drinking 125
 experiences 120-4
 food 125
 itineraries 116-17, 118-19, **116**, **118**
 shopping 125
 top experiences 114-15
 transport 111
 walking tours 116-17, 118-19, **116**, **118**
escape rooms 122
events 22-3

F

family travel 15, 69, 144
Ferris Wheel of Budapest 15, 82
festivals 22-3
Fisherman's Bastion 10-11, 15, 16, 41-2
food 18, 146-7, *see also* Eating *subindex*
Fröccsterasz 83
funicular 43

G

gay travellers 123-4, 148
Gellért Baths 6, 16, 19, 52-3
Gellért Hill 15, 16, 54-5
Gellért Hill & Tabán 49-61, **50-1**
 drinking 61
 experiences 58-60
 food 61
 itineraries 56-7, **56**
 shopping 61
 top experiences 52-5
 transport 49
 walking tours 56-7, **56**
Golden Eagle Pharmacy Museum 44
Gozsdu Courtyard 9, 121
Great Synagogue 17, 19, 114

H

health 149
Heroes' Square 10, 15, 17, 19, 138
HÉV travel 26
highlights 6-15, 36-9, 52-5, 62-3, 68-9, 90-3, 103, 114-15, 129-31, 138-41

hiking 12, 72
history 10-11
   1956 Uprising 28
   Roman Empire 68
   communism 13, 62-3, 115
   Memento Park 62-3
   World War II 115
Holocaust Memorial Centre 8, 129
Hospital in the Rock Nuclear Bunker Museum 19, 42-3
hostels 145
hotels 145
Houdini, Harry 97
House of Houdini 41, 43
House of Music 8, 141
House of Terror 14, 17, 19, 115
House of Unicum 135
Hungarian Museum of Trade and Hospitality 18, 19, 74
Hungarian National Gallery 8, 16, 19, 38-9, 38
Hungarian National Museum 19, 130-1
Hungarian Railway History Park 107
Hungarian State Opera House 10, 17, 97

I
ice-skating 13
itineraries 16-19

J
jazz 107, 135
Jewish Quarter, *see* Erzsébetváros & the Jewish Quarter

K
Kassák Museum 73
Kerepesi Cemetery 14, 63, 134
Kiscelli Museum 74

L
Labyrinth 44
language 154-5
LGBTIQ+ travellers 123-4, 148
Liberty Monument 16, 54-5
Liszt Ferenc Academy of Music 17, 120
Liszt Ferenc Memorial Museum 120
Liszt, Franz 28, 117, 120

literature 83
live music 9, 22, 60, 107, 124, 135
Lukács Baths 6, 73

M
Margaret Island 12, 103
Margaret Island & Northern Pest 101-9, **102**
   drinking 108-9
   experiences 106-7
   food 108
   itineraries 104-5, **104**
   shopping 109
   top experiences 103
   transport 101
   walking tours 104-5, **104**
markets 14, 17, 132-3, 135
   Nagycsarnok 17, 133
Memento Park 14, 62-3
metro travel 25
Miksa Róth Memorial House 121
Millennium Underground Museum 17, 82
money 21, 27, 146-7
Museum of Applied Arts 134
Museum of Ethnography 141
Museum of Fine Arts 8, 17, 19, 138
Museum of Music History 41, 44
museums 8, 23, 73, *see also individual museums*

N
National Museum 8, 17
New York Café 17, 19, 120
nightlife 9, 17, 147-8, *see also* Drinking *subindex*
Normafa 18, 72
Northern Pest, *see* Margaret Island & Northern Pest

O
Óbuda Museum 73
Óbuda Synagogue 74
Óbuda & the Buda Hills 65-75, **66-7**
   drinking 75
   experiences 72-4
   food 75
   itineraries 70-1, **70**
   top experiences 68-9

   transport 65
   walking tours 70-1, **70**
opening hours 147, 153
outdoor activities 12

P
Palace of Art 135, 141
Pál-völgy Cave 12, 72
parks & gardens
   Bottomless Lake 60
   City Park 12, 138-41, **140**
   Garden of Philosophers 55, 57
   Japanese Garden 106
   Károly Garden 83
   Memento Park 14, 62-3
   Normafa 72
Parliament 10, 16, 90-1
Parliament & Around 87-99, **88-9**
   drinking 99
   experiences 96-7
   food 98-9
   itineraries 94-5, **94**
   shopping 99
   top experiences 90-3
   transport 87
   walking tours 94-5, **94**
Pinball Museum 28, 107
planning 20-1
population 153
public holidays 153

R
responsible travel 150-1
Római-part 12, 74
Royal Palace 10, 15-16, 36-9
Rudas Baths 6, 58
ruin bars 9, 124

S
safe travel 149
security 149
Semmelweis Museum of Medical History 58
SkyDeck 60
Southern Pest 127-37, **128**
   drinking 136-7
   experiences 134-5
   food 136
   itineraries 132-3, **132**
   shopping 137
   top experiences 129-31
   transport 127
   walking tours 132-3, **132**

INDEX

street art 28-9, 122-3
surprises 28-9
sustainability 150-1
swimming 103
synagogues 19, 74, 114, 117
Széchenyi Baths 6-7, 28, 139
Szemlő-hegy Cave 12, 72
Sziget Festival 20, 22, 72
Szimpla Kert 9, 17, 124

T
Tabán, *see* Gellért Hill & Tabán
taxis 24, 26
thermal baths 6-7, 16-17, 19, 20, 28, 52-3, 58, 73, *see also individual baths*
time 21, 153
tipping 21, 146
toilets 153
train travel 24
   Keleti Railway Station 24, 123
   Nyugati Railway Station 24, 123
tram travel 13, 25
transport 24, 25-7
travelling with kids 15, 69, 144
travel seasons 22-3

V
Vajdahunyad Castle 19, 138-9
Városliget Lake 13, 140
vegetarian & vegan travellers 47, 61, 108, 137, 146
Veli Bej Baths 6, 73
Victor Vasarely Museum 18, 73

W
walking tours 40-1, 56-7, 70-1, 80-1, 94-5, 104-5, 116-17, 118-19, 132-3, **40, 56, 70, 80, 94, 104, 116, 118, 132**
waterparks 103
weather 22-3
wine 22, 96, 134

Eating

21 Magyar Vendéglő 46

A
Á Table 47
African Buffet 136
Amore di Napoli 61
Arany Kaviár 46
Aranybástya 46
Arquitecto Pitpit 136

B
Baalbek 84
Babka 108
Bigfish 98
Bombay Budapest 98
Borbíróság 136
Borkonyha 98
Budavári Rétesvár 47
Búsuló Juhász 55, 61

C
Café Kör 93, 98
Csalánosi Csárda 75

D
Daubner Cukrászda 75
Deszka 84

F
Felix Kitchen & Bar 61
Fény utca Market 46
Firkász 108

G
Geraldine 131
Gerlóczy Café 84
Gettó Gulyás 125
Giulia 46
Gundel 17

H
Hanoi Xua 136
Horgásztanya Vendéglő 46
Hummus Bar 75

J
Jin Galbi 98

K
Kéhli Vendéglő 18, 75
Kelet Café & Gallery 53
Kisharang 98
Kiskakukk 108
Kispiac Bisztró 98
Kőleves 125

M
Mák 98
Mandragóra 46
Marumba 125
Menza 125

Monk's Bistrot 84
Moto Pizza 61

N
Náncsi Néni 75
Normafa Síház 75

O
Öcsi 136
ODA 57, 61
Okay Italia 108
Okuyama no Sushi 75
Opium 98
Oriental Soup House 108

P
Paletta Bistró 136
Pavillon de Paris 46
Pest-Buda 46
Pick Bistro & Deli 91, 98
Pierrot 46
Pingrumba 46-7
Pizzica 98
Pozsonyi Kisvendéglő 108
Punjab Tandoori 108

R
Rosenstein 136
Royal Guard Restaurant & Cafe 37, 46
Ruben Restaurant 84
Ruszwurm Cukrászda 16, 37, 41, 47

S
Semmi Extra 75
Smokey Monkies 98
Solid 84
Stand25 46
Szeged Halászcsárda 84

T
Taverna Dionysos 84
Tefliso 136
Tokio Budapest 99
Trattoria La Coppola 84

U
UnoMas 108

V
Vegan Love 61

 Drinking

4 perc és kávé 47
360 Bar 18, 125

A
Alterego 99
Arch & Beans 85
Artizán 99

B
Babka Deli 109
Béla 61
Bereg Embassy Bar & Cafe 47
Blue Tomato 109
Bortodoor City 96

C
Café Csiga 136
Centrál Kávéház 84
Csendes Társ 84-5

D
DiVino Borbár 96
Dunapark 109

E
Edison & Jupiter 85
Élesztőház 137
Espresso Embassy 99

F
Fekete 85
Fellini Római 75
Figaró Kert 109

G
Gaby's 108
Garden Cafe 137
Geraldine 137

H
Hadik 61
Havana 125
Hippie Island 109

K
Kaledonia 99
Kelet Café & Gallery 61
Kert 75
Két Rombusz 75

L
Lánchíd Söröző 47

Leo Budapest 47

M
Macska 137
Mad Garden Óbuda 75
Mai Manó Cafe 99
Monyo Tap House 137
Morrison's 2 99
Mosselen 109

N
Nándor Cukrászda 137
Nem Adom Fel Kávézó és Étterem 137

O
Oinos 137
Ötkert 99

P
Palack Borbár 61
Párisi Passage Café & Brasserie 81, 84
Port de Budapest 85
Púder Bárszínház 136-7

S
Sarki Fűszeres 109
Savoyai Terasz 47
Smúz Cafe 99
St Andrea Skybar 18, 85
Steamhouse Cafe 47
Stifler Beerhouse & Kitchen 137
Stranger Cafe 109

T
Tilos a Tilos 136
Twentysix Budapest 125

V
Vaj 137

W
White Raven 41, 47
Why Not Cafe 85

Z
Zsiráf Tranzit 61

 Shopping

B
Bestsellers 99
Bortársaság 47

C
Cadeau 85

F
Folkart Kézművésház 85
Fromage 109

G
Gouba-Gozsdu bazár 125

H
Herend 41, 47
Holló Műhely 85

L
Ligeti Bolt 109
Liszt Ferenc Zeneműbolt 137
LoveChild Vintage 125

M
Magyar Pálinka Háza 137
Memories of Hungary 99
Mézes Kuckó 109

O
Originart Galéria 99

P
Paloma Artspace 85
Prezent 61

R
Retrock 125
Rododendron 85
Rózsavölgyi Csokoládé 85

S
Stühmer 109
Szputnyik Shop D-20 125

T
Taste the World 137

V
Vass Shoes 85

W
Wave Music 99

Z
Zsebi 109

Send Us Your Feedback

We love to hear from travellers – your comments help make our books better. We read every word, and we guarantee that your feedback goes straight to the authors. Visit lonelyplanet.com/contact to submit your updates and suggestions.

Note: We may edit, reproduce and incorporate your comments in Lonely Planet products such as guidebooks, websites and digital products, so let us know if you are happy to have your name acknowledged. For a copy of our privacy policy visit lonelyplanet.com/legal.

Acknowledgements

Cover photograph: Parliament (p90), Danube River. Richard Taylor/4Corners Images ©

Back photograph: Gellért Baths (p52). Stefano Ember/Shutterstock ©

THIS BOOK

Destination Editor
Sandie Kestell

Cartographer
Valentina Kremenchutskaya

Production Editor
Ailbhe MacMahon

Book Designer
Hannah Blackie

Assisting Editors
Andrew Bain, Clifton Wilkinson, Alison Killilea, Hannah Cartmel, Sasha Drew

Cover Researcher
Gerilyn Attebery

Thanks to
Ronan Abayawickrema, Sofie Andersen, Fergal Condon, Katerina Pavkova

Although the authors and Lonely Planet have taken all reasonable care in preparing this book, we make no warranty about the accuracy or completeness of its content and, to the maximum extent permitted, disclaim all liability arising from its use.

All rights reserved. No part of this publication may be copied, stored in a retrieval system, or transmitted in any form by any means, electronic, mechanical, recording or otherwise, except brief extracts for the purpose of review, and no part of this publication may be sold or hired, without the written permission of the publisher. Lonely Planet and the Lonely Planet logo are trademarks of Lonely Planet and are registered in the US Patent and Trademark Office and in other countries. Lonely Planet does not allow its name or logo to be appropriated by commercial establishments, such as retailers, restaurants or hotels. Please let us know of any misuses: lonelyplanet.com/legal/intellectual-property.

Paper in this book is certified against the Forest Stewardship Council™ standards. FSC™ promotes environmentally responsible, socially beneficial and economically viable management of the world's forests.

Published by Lonely Planet Global Limited
CRN 554153
6th edition – Jul 2025
ISBN 978 1 83758 366 9
© Lonely Planet 2025
Photographs © as indicated 2025
10 9 8 7 6 5 4 3 2 1
Printed in Malaysia